# THE HALAKHIC MIND

# THE
# HALAKHIC MIND

An Essay on
Jewish Tradition and Modern Thought

*Rabbi Joseph B. Soloveitchik*

## SETH PRESS

*Distributed by*

## THE FREE PRESS

*A Division of Macmillan, Inc.*
New York

*Collier Macmillan Publishers*
London
1986

Seth Press
Distributed by
The Free Press
A Division of Macmillan, Inc.
866 Third Avenue, New York, N.Y. 10022
Collier Macmillan Canada, Inc.


**Library of Congress Cataloging-in-Publication Data**

Soloveitchik, Joseph, Dov.
  The Halakhic mind.

  1. Religion—Philosophy.  2. Science-Philosophy.
3. Religion and science—1946-    .    4. Jewish law—
Philosophy, Jewish.  I. Title.
BL51.S6165    1986        296.3′875        86-6517
ISBN 0-02-930040-1

Printed in the United States of America
printing number
1 2 3 4 5 6 7 8 9 10

# Contents*

---

## THE HALAKHIC MIND

### PART ONE

### PART TWO

---

* Prepared by publisher

## Author's Note

This essay was written in 1944 and is being published for the first time, without any revisions or additions. The author wishes to thank Harold Rabinowitz of Seth Press for his valuable assistance in seeing this work through to publication.

PART ONE

# THE HALAKHIC MIND

# I

I T would be difficult to distinguish any epoch in the history of philosophy more amenable to the meditating *homo religiosus*[1] than that of today. The reason for this is the discrepancy that exists at present between the mathematico-scientific and philosophical methodologies. A schism of enormous magnitude has developed between the scientist and the philosopher, between the regional viewpoint of the empiricist and the universal vision of the metaphysician. The scientific method, which exalts the microscopic idea and integrates reality out of the simplest elements, has collided with the metaphysical world-view which strives towards boundless ontological totality. As a result of this conflict, new vistas now beckon to the *homo religiosus.*

From time immemorial, whenever the identity of the individual and community was shattered, man encountered God (e.g., the Paradisiacal man after his fall; Moses after the episode of the golden calf). Religious experience is born in crisis. The transcendental "adventure"—"the flight of the alone to the Alone"—is precipitated by despair. Man in his chancing upon the contradictory and absurd in life apprehends the vision of a hidden God—*deus absconditus.* Modern theology and philosophy of religion in their exposition of the supreme experience, draw continually upon Heraclitean-Hegelian[2] dialectical wisdom. If "faith is divine madness" and religion the great "paradox" of the crisis (Kierkegaard, Barth, Brunner, Otto) then the paradoxical present day conflict of science and philosophy and the crisis of the latter may yet give birth to a new religious world perspective.

Whenever scientist and philosopher agree, the *homo religiosus* is confronted with an *embarras de choix*. He must either develop an apologetic philosophy, or admit impotence in grasping the mystery of creation, or revolt against the hegemony of reason. When the *homo religiosus* turns apologetic, the rationalization of religion (scholasticism) is born. When he confesses ignorance, he turns agnostic and statements of *credo quia absurdum est* characterize his religious viewpoint. And when he revolts against reason, mysticism springs into being.

However, neither rationalistic complacency nor agnostic despair nor mystical rapture will yield a solution to the religious problem of modern man. The *homo religiosus* calmly but persistently seeks his own path to full cognition of the world. He claims freedom of methodology; he has faith in his ability to perform the miracle of comprehending the world; and notwithstanding the asymmetrical appearance of the *mysterium tremendum*, he eschews nonrational methods as a means to the realization of his goals.

However, it is only during times of contention between the mathematical sciences and philosophy that religion may avail itself of an autonomous attitude. And indeed, owing to many factors, a state of tension has prevailed between science and philosophy for many decades. (In the course of this essay, some of these factors will be enumerated.) As a result of this conflict, the whole complex of the philosophy of religion—methodology, circumscription of its object, categorical apparata, and cognitive aspects of the religious act—has been revised. For the *homo religiosus,* this might be justly perceived as a propitious turn of events.

## II

W HEN we speak of a conflict existing between philosophy and science, we do not have in mind a controversy concerning scientific data which philosophy would interpret in a manner alien to science. Modern philosophy neither pretends omniscience nor countenances the audacity to doubt in the least the validity of scientific statements. It is not inclined to repeat the fatal errors of the Hegelian school which attempted to defy the empiricist. Philosophy is well aware of the fact that it is impossible to derive scientific data from any *a priori* process of cognition. Nor is the issue between philosophy and science the problem of whether the scientist has the right to interpret phenomena in accord with his vantage point and method. The problem is, rather, whether the scientist's interpretation is to be exclusive, thus eliminating any other cognitive approach to reality. In other words, is the scientific interpretation to serve as the starting point for the philosopher whose object in such an instance would be a scientifically constructed universe, or does he have the prerogative of approaching reality from his own purview?

Let us analyze this controversy in the light of the history of philosophy. Great philosophical systems are never produced in a scientific vacuum, but usually follow the formation and completion of a scientific world-perspective. This priority of scientific knowledge to philosophical interpretation can be discerned twice in the history of philosophy: First, in the Aristotelian natural sciences and metaphysics, which dominated occidental thought throughout ancient and medieval times; and second, in the Galilean-Newtonian mathematical physics, which fostered the modern philosophy of nature. Aristotelian metaphysics and all other kindred *philosophema* reflect the peripatetic scientific approach to reality.[3] Modern philosophy, likewise, from Descartes to scientific positivism and Neo-Kantianism (the Marburg school) is nothing but an echo of the mechanistic physics which culminated in the Galilean-Newtonian interpretation of reality.[4] Aristotelian and Scholastic metaphysics, on the one hand, and modern philosophical criticism, scientific positivism and realism, on the other, regardless of their diametrical opposition, accepted an identical principle. Both adopted a scientifically purified world as the subject matter of their studies. The only realm of reality to which the philosopher had access was, for them, the scientifically charted universe.

Philosophy remained the satellite of science until the beginning of the twentieth century. Consistent with this, it distinguished between two world perspectives, the postulated and the "naive," glorifying the former and contemning the latter. The naive or "private" world interpretation, consisting of qualitative sense-data, was considered beyond philosophical bounds. It was deemed unworthy of the efforts of the philosopher, for its very ontological nature was denied. The philosophers of the Platonic and Aristotelian schools[5] had frowned upon the phenomenal and the particular, the only appearances accessible to our sense-perception; both of which were deemed unworthly of *noesis*. The noetic act could apprehend only the unchangeable, the eternal—the conceptual essence of being abstracted from the immediate, sensible and qualitative manifold. Similarly, modern philosophical criticism (Kantian and Neo-Kantian schools alike) and positivism also looked askance upon the qualitative world. Thus, the world comprising the sum total of our consciousness, the world of the senses, with which our very being is integrated, was rejected by these philosophical systems, as relativistic, subjective and ephemeral. Our variegated environment of qualitative flux was supplanted with abstract concepts and symbolic relational constructs. Both philosopher and scientist roamed a universe of quantitative relata and mathematical interdependencies. The postulated universe became the home of the philosopher. Exploring its infinite, uniform and metric lanes, he attempted to chart them. Locke's classification of primary and secondary qualities (formulated in consonance with Newton's physics) guided classical philosophers in their appraisal of reality. This act of surrender on the part of the philosopher to the omnipotence of science was not peculiar to any single school or shade of thought. The realist and the idealist,[6] the metaphysical spiritualist[7] and the materialist alike demonstrated loyalty to the empiricist and surveyed reality from scientific premises.[8]

As a matter of fact, it is worthy of note that the idealist, who deduced reality from knowledge, adhered more tenaciously to a scientifically postulated world than the realist. Although the latter, under the influence of positivistic tendencies, developed a doctrine of so-called scientific realism, he could nevertheless deviate from scientific, authoritative dicta. For he had faith in the existence of an absolute reality uncorrelated with any form of knowledge. Thus, while the realist apprehended reality from both the "public" scientific and the "private" naive viewpoints alike and was able to commit the "horrible" act of bifurcation, the idealist was compelled to accept a monistic being synonymous with knowledge. The former could afford the luxury of positing a phenomenal, qualitative reality without committing a *lèse majesté* against the absolute impenetrable

Being which remained beyond the pale of the cognitive act. The latter, however, who denied the existence of the Absolute and maintained the identity of reality with the "logos," could hardly be satisfied with ascribing ontological characteristics to the qualitative world. If reality is a creation of knowledge, as it is for idealistic philosophy, then scientific standards must be its exclusive measuring rods. Hence, idealistic philosophy displayed utter contempt for the private, sensory experience and dedicated itself solely to the elaboration of an abstract, conceptual world-image.

## III

AT the turn of the century, the harmony between the philosopher and scientist was disturbed. The dissonance arose out of the discovery that scientific data presented by biology and psychology clash with the forms set by the mathematical sciences which had been adopted by philosophy as the model of knowledge. Bergson was the first to become aware of the discrepancies prevailing between the problems of life and the consciousness and the basic philosophical methods couched in mathematical and physical concepts. The biological and psychical phenomena which then resisted (and still resist) a purely mechanistic explanation in the spirit of the physicist and chemist, portended a review of the traditional relationship which existed between science and philosophy. In his discussion on *Le Parallelisme Psychophysique et la Metaphysique Positive*[9] Bergson emphasized the fact that Kant, in his

*Critique of Pure Reason,* had not criticized reason as such, but reason fashioned to the habits and exigencies of the Cartesian mechanism or the Newtonian physic. "Let us ask," continues Bergson, "whether our metaphysics cannot be reconciled with science, simply because it lags behind science, being the metaphysics of a rigid science with entirely mathematical categories, in short, of the science that flourished from Descartes to Kant . . . while the science of the nineteenth century seems to have aspired to much more subtle form, and not always to have taken mathematics as its model."

Bergson not only discovered[10] the gap separating philosophy and biology but also undertook to bridge it. However, in his zeal to create a "Critique of Biological Reason," he did not suspect that several years later philosophy would lag not only behind biological problems, but ironically enough, even behind its mentor, physics. As a matter of fact, Bergson's biologistic crusade against philosophies shaped by physics, however prophetic and revolutionary, went unheeded even by biologists who, adhering preponderately to mechanistic doctrines, perceived no discrepancy between the physico-chemical domain and the realm of life. Bergson's philosophy was regarded as the rapturous outpouring of a mind obsessed with the autonomy of life. Even today this biological autonomy is still problematic, and certainly there were no real grounds at the beginning of the century, when science and philosophy were yet in accord, for any mathematical philosophy to fear the challenge of neo-vitalistic doctrines. The menace to classical mathematical philosophy did not emerge from the sphere of life, as Bergson thought, but paradoxically enough, from modern mathematical physics, where new aspects, such as non-Euclidian geometry, relativity and quantum mechanics, radically changed the entire scientific mode of thinking.

Mathematicians and physicists began expounding "heresies" that undermined the accepted principles of classical mathematics and physics. Postulates and theorems of apodictic value which had been canonized by science and philosophy alike now had to be reexamined and reinterpreted. Here scientific progressiveness and philosophical conservatism parted. Whereas science accepted these revolutionary innovations and began to revise its systematic explanation of reality, philosophy found itself nonplussed. The new scientific constructs were incompatible with philosophical methodology. They could neither be assimilated by modern philosophy, nor fitted into the traditional philosophical frame. Philosophy could not keep pace with the accelerated progress of scientific research. As a matter of fact, philosophy is not, as yet, fully cognizant of the new perspectives that have been disclosed in the various fields of mathematics and physics, perspectives which transcend the confines of the empirical and reach into the speculative and metaphysical. At the same time, it is nonetheless true that the basic concepts of theoretical philosophy, as posited by Descartes, Kant and other schools, in obeisance to modern science, are totally incommensurable with the new scientific constructs. The classical concepts of time, space, causality, quantity, substance, etc., are inadequate for interpreting the new vistas opened by the mathematical sciences.[11]

The "paradoxical" feature of this cleavage of scientific empiricism and philosophical speculation is that in contrast with other similar episodes in the history of knowledge, it originated with the philosopher and not with the physicist.

The relation between physicist and philosopher is different today from what it was during the period of classic mechanism. The mechanist of old was, at times, prone to jettison philosophical concepts and epistemological methods, arguing that the physical universe can be explained with the help of the simplest of formulae. He questioned the usefulness of philosophical thought which, rather than clarify, beclouds its ideas. In fact, modern skepticism and pragmatism (Mach, Avenarius, James, Peirce, Schiller, Vaihinger and others) which are acts of self-negation on the part of philosophy, are in a very real sense results of classical mechanics.

The modern physicist, however, does not ignore philosophical methods. The affinity between theoretical physics and epistemology is so strong today that certain outstanding physicists are inclined to assume that the demarcation line between these disciplines is almost nonexistent. The physical world-picture of today is incomplete without a philosophical frame. This unique need on the part of the empiricist for collaboration with the epistemologist has been brought about by the excessive physical formalism and symbolism of today. The postulated character of physical magnitudes is now more conspicuous than ever before. While Newtonian physics was compatible with our mathematico-physical intuition, and its postulated universe reflected our sensual environment, the modern physical world is beyond the range of man's intuitive faculty and sensibility. The passage from physical constructs to living, concrete phenomena is tortuous. Out of this remoteness of physical theory from subjective experience the need for philosophical interpretation emerged. Prodigal scientific abstraction requires epistemological implementation. However, there does not always exist a correspondence between scientific stimulus and philosophical response. Although the new concepts of space, time, substance, causality are, as yet, in need of philosophical formulation, the philosophy that would effectuate this is not in evidence. Newtonian physics found its philosophical apostle in Kant; modern physics is still awaiting its philosophical expounder.

## IV

IN view of these developments, the philosopher had to choose between admitting impotence in grasping the new ontological structure and deserting his master, the scientist. And, indeed, this dilemma in which epistemology suddenly found itself sundered the philosophical world. Old schisms were revived and assumed new meaning. Some philosophers continued to march humbly after the sciences, while others developed a non-scientific methodology. The first group, consisting of the so-called logical positivists, empiricists and physical realists (upon whom men like Poincaré, Mach, Avenarius, Russell, and White-head exercised great influence) limited the cognitive task of philosophy to the analysis of scientific concepts and methods. According to this school, metaphysical problems are pseudo-problems. Science alone has the exclusive right to cognition. Philosophy may only borrow finished products from the scientist's laboratory but has no right to participate in their fabrication. The medieval role of philosophy as handmaid was once again revived. But this time the handmaid must oblige a new mistress—Science.

The second group, consisting of insurgent metaphysicians and epistemologists, raised the banner of an independent philosophical methodology. These philosophers maintain that the positivistic school, in unconditionally accepting scientific dicta, reduces itself to an ancillary discipline of theoretical physics. And, indeed, while classical philosophy succeeded in producing a philosophical exposition of postulated reality, contemporary scientific positivism has not been very effective in its attempt at interpreting the physical universe. Positivism of today is servile to science. It accepts scientific statements without analysing them critically. Philosophical pride has prompted metaphysicians to venture forth on a new non-scientific road and proclaim the renaissance of a philosophical world-interpretation. These philosophers suddenly became aware that apart from a quantitative universe there exists a qualitative one that has never been explored by classical philosophy. The variegated, colorful world, which for so long had remained in primordial loneliness, became, within a relatively short time, the favorite haunt of the philosopher. The world intriguing the contemporary philosopher is not that which is "public" and constructed, but the "private," intuited one.[12]

In justifying such an approach, the argument of the philosopher runs more or less as follows: The implements of science enable the scientist to deal solely with those aspects of reality capable of quantification. Qualities themselves are too elusive and intangible to be caught in the scientist's mesh. But, says the contemporary philosopher, this does not necessarily imply that the method of atomization and quantification of specific sense qualities employed by the scientist in his laboratory need be considered the exclusive approach to reality. Perhaps there are many keys to the ontological kingdom. Let us take (he continues) Bergson's efforts, for example. Whatever the shortcomings of Bergson's biologistic philosophy, one cannot overemphasize the influence he wielded upon the emergence of new criteria in philosophy's encounter with the spirit. The humanistic sciences gained thereby methodological independence. Since then, through the efforts of men like William James, Dilthey, Eucken, Boutroux, *et al.*, methodologies in the realm of the humanistic sciences have emancipated themselves from the mechanistic bondage; new trails have been blazed in the wilderness of mental subjectivity.

What has transpired in the humanistic sciences, continues the philosopher, should be emulated in the philosophical domain. If Bergson and others pointed, for instance, at the time concept and demonstrated the discrepancies prevalent between the time awareness of the physicist (who freezes time in geometric space) and that of the psychologist (who intuits time as living and creative), then why should not the philosopher evolve a time principle suited to his own needs and aspect? A similar pluralism may be discerned in other categories as well, as, for example, in causality, which is interpreted differently by the physicist and humanist. Hence, the alleged homogeneity of the logical category was but a naive illusion on the part of the classical philosopher. Sober epistemological facts demonstrate the heterogeneity and pluralistic character of the most basic cognitive methods.[13] The physical aspect is but one of many.

As a matter of fact, the foregoing argument is warranted by the later advancement of an independent humanistic methodology. Contrary to all naturalistic and positivistic attempts (including classical associationism and modern behaviorism) to subserve the spirit to the quantifying methods of the scientist, the humanistic sciences have developed specific independent standards. Whether spirit and nature are indeed two different domains, as averred by the proponents of ontic duality (*extensio* and *cogitatio*), or whether mind and external being copenetrate in a monistic fashion is irrelevant to the methodologist. The fact has been ascertained beyond any doubt that instruments which measure *extensio* are neither universal, omnipotent nor applicable to the spirit. The humanistic sciences, therefore, have reexamined all categories and principles of theoretical philosophy formed under the hegemony of the modern mathematical sciences. They have discovered that the classical categorial system had been constructed purely to suit the scientist, while the unique aspects of the internal world were entirely ignored. The modern humanistic sciences have rejected positivistic interpretations of the spirit (in terms of mechanics and electromagnetism) and have shaped a methodology of their own.

Of course, the argument of the philosopher, which takes the humanistic autonomous methodology as a precedent, may be attenuated by contending that the duality of methodological aspects in regard to nature and spirit is warranted by ontological factors alone. Externality and inwardness, whether interpreted dualistically or monistically, still present two appearances of reality. The temperament in which we meet nature is different from the one in which we approach our own mind. The crux of the question is, rather, what justifies a duality of cognition within nature or within the spirit itself?

To this the philosopher will reply that heterogeneity is inherent not only within reality as a whole—thus dividing it into two unique domains, the corporeal and spiritual—but also within each of its segments. Many singular facts reveal the ontological mystery to baffled man, who, at times, doubts the very unity and identity of reality. The qualitative and quantitative aspects are but two of a manifold. The old Spinozistic vision of an infinite substance, manifest through an endless number of attributes, out of which *extensio* and *cogitatio* are the only ones accessible to our mind, was not an idle dream. Our pluralistic cognitive approach is warranted by such ontological heterogeneity; and the philosopher may gain access to reality in a manner alien to the physicist or biologist.

Methodology, the contemporary metaphysician further maintains, is determined not only by ontological aspects but also by axiological and teleological considerations presented by Being itself. Modern axiology plays a major role in this respect. Every system of cognition strives to attain a distinct objective. Systematic knowledge means the understanding and grasping of the universe in consonance with a definite telos. It is interested primarily that reality reveal itself in a fashion which is suited to a final noetic goal; the telos is the determining factor in the methodological construction employed by the scientist and philosopher. Teleological heterogeneity, however, does not invalidate the cognitive act, for, in the final analysis, pluralism is founded on reality itself. It is important to note that this trend of thought has nothing in common with operational pragmatism. While pragmatism, in its essence, is positivistic[14] and annuls the idea of the absolute, epistemological pluralism does not deny the absolute character of Being. On the contrary, it is ontologically conscious of, and reserves a central position in its perspective for, absolute reality. Pluralism asserts only that the object reveals itself in manifold ways to the subject, and that a certain *telos* corresponds to each of these ontical manifestations. Subsequently, the philosopher or scientist may choose one of the many aspects of reality in compliance with his goal.[15]

PART TWO

# THE HALAKHIC MIND

# I

THE emergence of pluralistic trends is strikingly manifest in all modern metaphysical endeavors that strive
for the mysterious Absolute. Whatever the realm of the
Absolute—the Whole and Individual (Bradley, Bosanquet,
Royce), non-existent eternal essences (Husserl, Santayana),
or absolute values and norms (Lotze, Windelband)—one
postulate is clear, namely, the method of approach is non-
scientific. And the reason for this is obvious. Every
metaphysical quest for reality is driven by the urge for
finality and totality which neither scientific microscope nor
telescope can reveal. Thus, the absolute perspective of ontology must remain intrinsically non-scientific. In addition,
metaphysics can never be satisfied with merely theoretical
considerations, however absolute their character may be,
but must weave axiological threads into its philosophical
fabric, whereas science is indifferent to value-judgements
and ethical norms. The Kantian and Neo-Kantian undertaking to separate the theoretical reason from the practical,
by constructing a philosophical triad of logic, ethics and
aesthetics, gives no comfort to the philosopher. Ontology
and axiology overlap and merge into one harmonious
whole. Bradley justly saw in the Absolute the unity and
synthesis of all modes of experience: rational, volitional
and sentimental. As soon as the philosopher turns to ends
and designs in the universe, he severs all ties with the
scientific method of interpretation and embraces
methodological pluralism. Thus, the non-scientific aspects

of modern philosophy are necessitated by the metaphysical urge of the thinker.[16]

Aside from the metaphysical schools which have a pluralistic attitude, certain anti-metaphysical schools (namely, pragmatic postivism and critical idealism) have also arrived at the same conclusions. At first glance, it would appear absurd that the philosophies which sprang into being under the aegis of the natural sciences should have deviated from their historical course and made inroads into the fields of cognitive pluralism. Yet, such a metamorphosis was warranted by certain encroaching philosophical realities with which the strictest scientific philosophy had to reckon.

As for pragmatism, William James bears testimony to this philosophic detour.[17] Albeit his position was the very antipode of ontological metaphysics, he nevertheless aligned himself with the metaphysicians of the Absolute against mathematico-scientific monopoly.[18] Under the impact of new aspects that emerged in the psychology of religion which had begun to beat a path through the brush and shrub of the religious consciousness, and under the magic spell of Bergson's biologism, James discovered a multi-dimensional cognitive aspect and arrived at the threshold of a "Pluralistic Universe." The positivistic pragmatic school maintains that, if categories and concepts such as substance, causality, reality, necessity, etc., are nothing but arbitrary creations of thought designed to order or classify the unknown, and if the guiding motives of the cognitive process are pragmatic considerations, there can be no objection to other approaches to reality, even though these be non-scientific. If the logical worth or "reality" of any world formula is measured by its "efficiency in doing its work" (Dewey) and in its performing "most felicitously its functions of satisfying our double urgency," the personal and objective (James), then there can be no reason why aspects alien to science should not be introduced into the cognitive field. Methodology is determined not by ontological principles but by the practical end; and the most objective methodology is the one that best serves the ends of a unified system. Pragmatism, therefore, has only to demonstrate a multitude of ends in order to legitimate a methodological manifold. Whether reality requires monistic or pluralistic interpretation is irrelevant, since all constructs, including the scientific, are but subjective addenda to the pure data. Hume's skepticism, which found its modern analogue in pragmatism, is the most convenient theory for epistemological pluralism.[19]

For critical idealism Cassirer speaks. This Neo-Kantian philosopher of symbolic forms, who, true to his Neo-Kantian traditions, scoffed at the idea of Absolute reality, while passionately believing in the intrinsic necessity and objectivity of the emergent "logos," had the least ground for casting aside his monistic doctrine. And yet, new scientific trends and revolutionary philosophical aspects have exerted irresistible fascination upon him, luring him away from his orthodox pan-rationalistic ideology. While classical Neo-Kantianism had unlimited faith in the monistic character of the cognitive process, conceiving the Creator of the universe as mathematician and physicist, the symbolistic philosophy discarded the monistic principle and embraced a pluralistic "religion." According to this school, the mind approaches the world with a multitude of aspects, each entailing implicit necessity and regularity. Language, myth, art, science and religion focus upon reality from their various symbolic perspectives, and none of them can lay claim to superiority in adequacy and validity.[20] The worship of

the deity of scientific law, most characteristic of the origina-
tors of Neo-Kantianism, has been transferred by such as
Cassirer to a multitude of cognitive idols. Thus, the three
schools which were considered inexorably hostile to each
other, absolute idealism which clamoured for the οντος ογ,
critical idealism which served the "logos", and pragmatism
which derided both, met on the common ground of
pluralism.

## II

APART from the separation of philosophy and science
and the rise of the humanistic methodology, a new
factor contributed to the emergence of an autonomous
philosophy, namely, the natural sciences themselves.

Modern epistemology became aware that scientists themselves differ in their employment of categorical apparata.[21]
To illustrate, the category of substance is applied differently
by the physicist and chemist. Although there is a definite
tendency to convert modern chemistry into a purely quantitative mathematico-scientific discipline,[22] the chemist nevertheless finds great difficulty in eschewing qualitative elements in his subject matter. He stands much closer to the
natural world than does the physicist. And this is even
more so in the case of the biologist. Neo-vitalistic theories
substantiate the incompatibility of the biological phenomena with abstractly postulated quantitative standards.

Similarly, the mathematician and physicist part company
on the question of the categorical formative approach.
Thus, as Poincaré indicated, the concept of space is vari-

ously interpreted by the mathematician and physicist. Whereas the former conceives space as pure extension, the latter sees in it the *real* background of the cosmic process. The problem of an empty or non-empty space, although irrelevant to the mathematician, is of prime importance to the physicist. Modern geometry, on the one hand, and the theory of relativity on the other, make this contrast more conspicuous. While modern geometry abandoned the classical determinate subject matter of geometry ("real" space) and operates with formal relations,[23] relativity integrated space with the actual cosmic occurrence. According to this theory, "space is no longer the stage upon which the drama of physics is being performed, for gravitation, which is a physical property, is entirely controlled by curvature, which is a geometrical property of space."[24] Space casts off the Newtonian dispensation of passivity and vacuity and is converted into an active participant in the physical drama.[25] What is more, the mere fact that modern geometry (or geometries) developed various equally valid space structures (Euclidean and non-Euclidean) attests to a pluralism inherent in the geometric manifold.

Methodological heterogeneity asserts itself likewise in certain procedures of modern quantum mechanics. While classical and relativity physics employed a rigid principle of geometrization, namely, a three (space) or four (space-time) dimensional continuum, quantum and wave mechanics enjoy greater freedom. The latter applies geometric standards which serve best the understanding of the physical universe. It uses a fictitious hyper-space, "the number of whose dimensions rises indefinitely with the number of the particles constituting the system under consideration."[26] It would appear that there are many numerical codes to which physical quantities can be assigned. Thus, the methodological differences which come to light in the application of the basic categories indicate a plurality of aspects under which reality may be viewed. The whole categorical system displays heterogeneity rather than uniformity.

What is perhaps most striking in all these considerations is that the physicist himself, in expounding "peculiar" epistemological theories concerning the physical world, has helped deliver the philosopher from his bondage to the mathematical sciences. Niels Bohr, in an attempt to interpret in epistemological terms, the mechanical laws of conservation of momentum and energy in the light of Heisenberg's Principle of Indeterminacy, developed his so-called theory of Complementarity (*Komplementaritaetstheorie*) which is, perhaps, more an epistemological than a physical doctrine. According to this theory, there is a dualistic approach to the physical universe—the spatio-temporal and the causalistic. Paradoxically enough, both aspects, although complementary in theoretical exposition, are nevertheless mutually exclusive when formulated mathematically. We may either satisfy ourselves with minute spatio-temporal determination, thus neglecting a precise, causalistic interpretation; or relegate the former to a statistical rank and explain the latter in accurate relational terms. Thus, the rigid laws of conservation, which have meaning only insofar as momentum and energy can be defined precisely, render impossible accurate localization of the same energy in space-time. The dualism of spatio-temporal and causalistic functions is crystallized into the theoretical dichotomy concerning the physical structure of light and matter. The two-fold approach to light, the wave and quantum viewpoints, represent the spatio-temporal and causalistic aspects respectively. Both are indispensable for a complete physical picture. However, as regards precise mathematical formulation, they are mutually exclusive.

In addition to his theory of Complementarity, Bohr, exploiting Heisenberg's Principle of Indeterminacy, undertook the refutation of the time-hallowed myth of the insularity of the objective world. The reciprocal relation of phenomenon and experiment and the interference of the latter (the light beam) with the objective occurrence of the former (the state of the particle) as implied in the principle of Indeterminacy, must remit the entire classic relation of subject-object for reconsideration; the claim of the natural sciences to absolute objectivity must undergo a thorough revision. What is more, Bohr sees an analgous approach by both the physicist to the external world and the psychologist to the internal world. Both, whether experimenting with physical or with mental states, must affect their objects by their very act of observing. The pristine object, when intercepted by the experimenter, is transformed, chameleon-like, from transcendent imperviousness to immanent merger with the subject.[27]

Among modern physicists, Bohr is not the only "traitor" to physicalism and positivism. Planck speaks unequivocally of the symbolic (and, alas, arbitrary!) logical constructs of the physicist who, to overcome the transient and elusive flux of the qualitative world, finds refuge in postulated abstractions and conceptual relations.[28] The father of quantum mechanics frankly stated that, while classical physics somehow found a passage from the physical universe to our familiar environment, modern physics is unable to translate scientific symbols into a working language for our sense-given world.

Einstein treats this subject in a similar vein.[29] He recognizes with Kant the spontaneous role of the "logos" in "creating" the conceptual instruments that are necessary for the scientific interpretation of reality.[30]

> The following, however, appears to me to be correct in Kant's statement of the problem: in thinking we use, with a certain 'right', concepts to which there is no access from the material of sensory experience, if the situation is viewed from the logical point of view. As a matter of fact, I am convinced that even much more is to be asserted: the concepts which arise in our thought and our linguistic expressions are all—when viewed logically—the free creations of thought which cannot inductively be gained from sense experiences. This is not so easily noticed only because we have the habit of combining certain concepts and conceptual relations (propositions) so definitely with certain sense experiences that we do not become conscious of the gulf, logically unbridgeable, which separates the world of sensory experiences from the world of concepts and propositions.

Needless to say, Eddington,[31] who never reconciled the mystic and philosopher with the physicist in himself, could find no satisfaction in "symbolic knowledge" or in a "world of shadows." He yearned for that "intimate knowledge" which supposedly redeems the consciousness from scientific provincialism and formalism. An ultra metaphysician of idealistic strain, seeking a cosmos *morphé* of harmony and beauty, lectures to us in "defense of mysticism" and on the "limitations of physical schemes," in the disguise of a mathematician and astronomer.

It is evident that the chorus of philosophical positivists and physicalists who sing Hallelujahs to our omniscient senses and benevolent Nature is drowned out by the answering refrain of the fathers of modern physics. Yet, when we read positivistic literature, we are confronted with an amusing situation. While the fathers of modern physics regard their own constructs with skeptical reservation, the enthusiastic positivists attribute final veracity to them. However, the opinion of the builders of modern physics is decisive, and *volens nolens* philosophy will have to adjust itself to certain epistemological changes.

It is apparent that the physicist who wants to formulate philosophically the results of his own scientific investigation is faced with a three-fold possibility. First, following Mach, he may reduce knowledge to inadequate, ancillary, subjective principles and deny the objective character of the postulated world. Second, he may apply the Kantian transcendental method and declare the complex of postulated concepts to be indispensable to the emergence of a scientifically regulated experience, thus legitimating their objectivity and logical necessity (as Planck and Einstein did.) Third, he may admit, with Eddington, that the scientist, arriving at the border of symbolic and absolute knowledge, must relinquish his prerogatives to the philosopher or mystic.

At present, the philosopher is little inclined to subscribe to a monistic Kantian or Neo-Kantian attitude. If the 'logos' is spontaneous, and if its freedom of cognitive postulation harmonizes with the logical norm of objectivity, then there can be no valid reason for the monopolization of creativity by the mathematical sciences. In such a case, other noetical designs may emerge that are as genuinely logical as the scientific relational aspect.[32] The net result of these considerations is that the vision of an independent philosophy begins to loom brightly on the cognitive horizon. The philosopher needs but a little audacity and courage.

What is the philosophic alternative to these pluralistic conclusions? One might offer skeptical pragmatism as a solution, but it is rather improbable that modern man, weary of changing standards and values, would accept the relativistic pragmatic gospel. At any rate, cognitive pluralism has a good case.[33] If this is so, why could not philosophy view the world from its own aspect and interpret it in harmony with its own needs and objectives?


## III

EPISTEMOLOGICAL pluralism encounters a two-fold problem: First, whether a non-scientific methodology is warranted by epistemological postulates, second, if indeed it is warranted, what is the specific structure of such a methodology?

Contemporary pluralistic philosophy of a pragmatic and critical strain has considered the first problem but ignored the second. It asserts that reality may be interpreted under a manifold of cognitive aspects. Methods adjust themselves to particular cognitive viewpoints; concepts are formed and categories shaped in accordance with a specific perspective delimited by the observer. However, pragmatic and critical pluralism remain mute as to the specific nature of the chosen methodology.

The reason for this evasion is that both pragmatism and symbolism deny the "existence" of a mysterious, pluralistic Absolute. Pluralism in knowledge does not correspond to an ontic manifold. Pragmatism and symbolism have never admitted an aspect of reality which might be grasped exclusively by an autonomous non-scientific method (as the phenomenologist and Neo-Hegelian said of the Absolute). Hence, these schools have pointed only to the possibility of disparate cognitive interpretations of the same object. But they have never taken the effort to develop more than one interpretation. If Being is either a myth of our subjective mind or a creation of the "logos," then the curiosity driving man to pluralistic knowledge is not irrepressible. The pragmatist and symbolist were satisfied with just one interpretation out of many. Thus, these philosophers unlocked the portals of a pluralistic universe but did not venture in.

Modern metaphysicians, however, were more daring and ambitious. Not only did they speak of pluralism but they also sought to develop a unique metaphysical method which would vouchsafe them a glimpse into the ontological *mysterium magnum*. The reason for the aggressiveness of the metaphysician where both pragmatist and critical idealist showed reticence is a two-fold one. First, the metaphysician faced a problem less intricate than that of his critical and positivistic antagonists. While their problem was pluralism, his was dualism,[34] scientific and philosophic—scientific in reference to phenomena and philosophical in regard to noumena. This dualistic formula saved him from the pluralistic maze and encouraged him to construct a new method.

Second, the noetical drive of the metaphysician is an overwhelming one. The romantic quest for the ontical nebulae lying in the outer fringes of the "here and now" reality spurs the philosopher on irresistibly to explore the domain of the Absolute. Thus, modern metaphysicians, such as Bradley, Royce, Bergson, Husserl and Max Scheler, the prophets of the Whole, Individual and Absolute, the traces of which reveal themselves in the sensuous, phenomenal reality, devoted the major part of their efforts to the formulation of a metaphysical methodology. Intuition, eidetic apprehension and emotional apriorism served as points of departure for the modern metaphysician.

Modern metaphysicians did not create their methodology *ex nihilo*. In fact, the new methods evolved by them were not new at all. They merely changed aspects; the natural-scientific was superseded by the humanistic. Instead of viewing reality from the standpoint of nature, they undertook to grasp it from that of the spirit. Hegel's methodology, based upon the autonomy of the mind, has become the elixir of modern metaphysicians. Their motto is: if nothing can be accomplished with the instruments of natural sciences, let us apply other standards which may yield positive results. The emergence of the modern humanities stimulated these proclivities still further. Late metaphysicians such as the phenomenologists and existentialists have exploited the humanistic standards for metaphysical purposes.[35]

Descriptive psychology (Dilthey),[36] with its method of understanding leading to the sympathetic fusion of object-subject, was adopted by all schools of modern metaphysics in order to grasp the unknown Absolute world order. To give a clear concept as to what these schools intended by a specific philosophical methodology, the methodological differences between physics and modern humanistic sciences must be examined. In summary, these are as follows:

I. The scientist conceives the unknown as an aggregate of simple elements. In order to apprehend nature, he must break down this intricate composite into its components. For example, when Galileo first began to lay the foundations of mechanics, he operated with concepts of ideal elementary motion. However, in reality, actual motion never occurs under the conditions which Galileo hypothesized when constructing his concept of ideal motion. Real motion is looked upon as the integrated results of many infinitesimal ideal elements. Such an additive approach was particularly epitomized in Newton, who enunciated the laws of motion in the form of differential equations and their integrations. The method of science is that of atomization and piecemeal summation.

II. Although classical physics assumed that all physical processes are endowed with continuity, which finds its mathematical expression in differential equations (even modern physics, which broke with the classical postulate of continuity, still speaks of a "probability fluid"), physics, nevertheless never apprehended reality's "thickness" as a continuum. The relational-continuous surface, which physics treats, has little in common with the metaphysical concept of continuity. The scientist merely dots the path of appearances; he is unable to create a perfect continuity. The world of the mathematician, Bergson once said, dies in the intervals and is born in the t-th moment that is relevant to the system. The scientist plots his course by substituting relational complexity for absolute continuous unity.

III. Knowledge, for science, is not concerned with content but form, not with the "what" but with the "why" and "how." It does not investigate A and B, but attempts to determine the interdependencies of these relata. A and B, as such, are nothing more than ideal points which serve the scientist as a means to the examination of inter-relations, just as the single terms in a series serve the mathematician in determining the character of that series.

IV. Recently, from the time of Hertz, Poincaré and Mach, to Einstein, Planck and Eddington, physics has begun to regard itself a postulated discipline of pure constructs and symbols correlated with the given. Copy realism with its *camera obscura*, claiming to photograph reality, has been abandoned. Knowledge of reality entails the construction of some ideal order coordinated with the qualitative cosmic process which retains its anonymity and mystery. The physicist substitutes an objective, ideally-constructed correlative for the inaccessible subjective experience of reality.

V. A scientific law is universal and refers to the genus as a whole.[37] The mathematical sciences operate with universals and not with particulars. Physics is intrinsically an abstract conceptual discipline. Modern science is the legal heir of Platonic, Aristolelian and medieval scholastic conceptual realism. Nominalistic trends have always led to skepticism and agnosticism.

VI. The controversy of antiquity between the Eleatic school of Parmenides, who denied change and accepted identical selfhood, and Heraclitus, who identified being with ceaseless motion and eternal flux, was adjudicated by science in favor of Parmenides. Both Newtonian and modern physics, although denying Zeno's contention concerning the absurdity of motion, have nevertheless constructed basic physical magnitudes of matter and force which display, in their basic and complex appearance, Eleatic traits. The classic principles of the indestructibility of matter and the conservation of energy, the modern principle of the conservation of mass-energy, and the character of time-space coordinates, in both classical and modern physics,[38] harmonize with the Eleatic attitude.

This position was adopted for two valid reasons: First, the postulated physical universe, consisting of relational constructs and numerical symbols, is immune to any metamorphosis of metaphysical strain. The scientific index registers only the metric character of the universe formulated in a functional system. Regardless of our experience of a changing reality, the relational world, formulated into mathematical equations, cannot be shaken, by any natural cataclysm. The numerical values placed upon the incomprehensible, qualitative phenomena display no susceptibility to an ever modulating "private" world.

Second, the concept of time with which physics operates renders "becoming" an impossibility within the bounds of the physical cosmos. Change and "becoming" presuppose a *conditio sine qua non* of an unalterable, directed succession of time—an arrangement of temporal instants on a scale of "before" and "after" that are not interchangeable. Events must run from an irreversible past into an anticipated future. Such unfolding of time in a one-way direction is the necessary antecedent of "becoming." Physics, however, does not know of such a time concept.[39] The cosmic process, as conceived by the physicist, is reversible. Its movement can progress from A to B and vice versa from B to A. Physical processes as described by classical and modern laws, can (in any conservative system) retrace their course. Future and past point to plus and minus directions which can be explored simultaneously. Hence, reversibility precludes the possibility of "change."

In contrast with these six cardinal scientific aspects, the humanistic hermeneutics constructed six antipodes:

I. The humanistic sciences presuppose the idea of wholeness and attempt to understand single processes in its light. The first impetus to the philosophical structural interpretation of reality came from Bergson in his attempt to formulate a "Critique of the Reason of the Biological Sciences." The organic and biologistic approach entails (as Bergson thought and as the Neo-Vitalists still maintain) the concept of the whole. Bergson, together with James[40] and others, abandoned psychological associationism or atomism and pointed to the aboriginal personality as a unifying principle. Hypotheses like mind, selfhood, consciousness, ego, stream of consciousnesss, psychological duration, Gestalt and the subconscious were substituted for the clusters of mental atoms of classical psychology. From psychology, the concept of the whole was carried over to the other humanistic sciences. Aggregates were replaced by primitive wholes.

II. The idea of "wholeness" gave the problem of continuity a new aspect. This problem must remain metaphysically insoluble as long as the physicist endeavors to create an additive whole out of simple elements. However, as soon as the psychologist or historian intuits the primitive configuration, a continuum is posited a priori.

III. The methodologist of the humanistic sciences is not interested in the genetic or historical problem of the "why" or "how" but in the functional problem of "what." The psychologist and historian penetrate the "thickness" of their object rather than survey its relational surface. The infinite distance separating the comprehending subject from the comprehended object is bridged. Object and subject fuse and become one. The meaningful content and structure of A and B and not their relational character is the outstanding problem of the humanist. The guiding star is no longer causality but the eidetic content and meaningful whole.

IV. By eliminating the relational criterion from the cognitive act and viewing spiritual reality from the aspect of "endosmosis as a conflux of the same with different,"[41] the humanist is preserved from the sin of "bifurcation" of reality. He does not duplicate reality by constructing an ideal order corresponding to the primordial qualitative realm. He is determined to capture the natural sensible reality in its full uniqueness.

V. The humanist is concerned not only with the conceptual and universal, but with the concrete particular and individual. Mental reality is characterized by uniqueness and otherness. By reducing spiritual reality to common denominators, we *eo ipso* empty it of its content. Bergson defined intuition as follows: "By intuition is meant the kind of intellectual sympathy, by which one places oneself within an object in order to coincide with what is unique in it and consequently inexpressible."[42] The concept can never replace individualities, structures which elude conceptual abstraction.

VI. Spiritual reality is a process of "becoming." There is nothing static in it; it is a continuous flux and conflux of qualitative movements. The term, "stream of consciousness," introduced into modern literature by William James, indicates the fleeting character of the human psyche. While the chief method of physical sciences is spatialization (time is frozen in geometric space and quantified by physical chronometry), the spiritual process eschews all externality and the consciousness emerges as a free and spontaneous agent. Such a viewpoint is akin to the Heraclitean vision of eternal flux.[43]

As has been stressed, philosophy, attempting to enter the domain of the Absolute, to which science has no access, perforce employed the humanistic method. Indeed, all claims of the modern metaphysician to have discovered a new method of interpreting 'the unknown' are without foundation.[44] The phenomenologist will, of course, object strenuously to such a reproach. He will assert that his method of apprehending the *essentiae* (*Wesensschau*) is both original and autonomous. He will point to the fact that he considers the Absolute as essences, universal and immutable, resembling in these characteristics the basic magnitudes of the scientific world-structure. Yet, a careful scrutiny of his methodology will lead us to the conclusion that his approach is similar to that of the humanist in two fundamental features. Both the ideas of "wholeness"[45] and "whatness" reign supreme in phenomenological philosophy. *Wesensschau* is nothing but the act of intuiting the essence under the aspect of the "whole" and the "what." Modern metaphysicians have merely borrowed the method of the humanistic sciences and applied it in the realm of the Absolute. Classical naturalism (although not always identical with materialism) endeavors to interpret the spirit from the premises of nature. "Independent" philosophy (although not always synonymous with spiritualism) reverses the method and attempts to grasp nature from the viewpoint of the spirit.

PART THREE

# THE HALAKHIC MIND

I

IT must be apparent that owing to such trends in general philosophy, the philosophy of religion has undergone radical changes. As long as general philosophy explored a quantitatively constructed universe, the philosophy of religion could not progress. The construction of a religious Weltanschauung in a world of quanta and mathematical interdependencies was impossible. The *homo religiosus* is little inclined to accept conceptual abstractions and quantitative transfigurations. It is for this reason that negative theologies have completely failed to impress the mind of God-worshippers.

Indeed, not even Maimonides succeeded in his attempt to purge Jewish liturgy of poetic elements and anthropomorphic symbols derived from our sensational experience. His endeavor to raise the prayer book to the lofty peaks of philosophical abstraction failed abysmally. Jewish God-worshippers have ignored the teaching of their master, Maimonides, and still sing hymns teeming with poetic refrain drawn from the well of human passion and emotion. Moreover, Jewish liturgists were not inclined to dispense even with anthropomorphic metaphors that lend warmth and color to the personal man–God relation. The practical God-worshipper considers any speculative interpretation of God as a religious nirvana. It is not the "logos" but the psycho-physical man who sings of God and His Glory. There is no longing for God in the metaphysical highlands where stoic calm prevails. By his nature, the worshipper is lured on irresistibly, from time to time by grotesquely anthropomorphic and figurative attributes. He begs the Almighty for a guiding hand, a friendly eye and a forgiving smile.[46]

The *homo religiosus* moves in a concrete world full of color and sound. He lives in his immediate, qualitative environment, not in a scientifically constructed cosmos. Hence, as long as cognition was the exclusive privilege of the scientist (and of the philosopher who followed in his traces), the *homo religiosus* sought a haven in other spheres. Theories of sentimental (Rousseau Schleiermacher) and ethico-volitional (Kant, Fichte, Cohen) origin gave substance to the religious experience. However, by accepting pluralistic interpretations of reality, philosophy released the *homo religiosus* from his fetters and encouraged him to interpret the polychromic and polyphonic appearances impinging upon him, the one of his psychosomatic being. In contrast with the scientist, the *homo religiosus* is unable to bifurcate reality; the world he knows is identical with the world he experiences.

The *homo religiosus* must regain his position in the cognitive realm. He is no longer the emotional creature, swayed by abstruse sentiments and ephemeral feelings; nor is he the ethical idealist in eternal quest for sanction and authority. He is a cognitive type, desiring both to understand and interpret. Reality, as the object upon which the cognitive act is directed, can no longer be the concern of the scientist and philosopher only, but also that of the *homo religiosus*. This does not mean that religion is about to repeat the errors of the Middle Ages and compete with science. It signifies only that knowledge is not the exclusive province of the theoretician of science; religion, too, has a cognitive approach to reality. Religious experience is not only of emotional or ethical essence, but is also deeply rooted in the noetic sphere. Indeed, the urge for *noesis* is of the very essence of religion.[47]

The philosophy of religion, however, faces another barrier which it must hurdle before it enters the theoretical domain. In the aforegoing, we have considered the noetic problems of religion from the *quid juris* standpoint—what warrants the cognitive venture of the *homo religiosus*. As to this problem, epistemological pluralism gives a satisfactory answer. Now the *quid facti* problem arises: wherein is the proof that there is an implicit cognitive function in the religious act? After all, there is no direct logical connection between epistemological pluralism and the cognitive character of religion. The fact that the philosopher and the humanist gained an autonomous access to reality does not *eo ipso* prove that cognitive tendencies are intrinsic to the religious act. The noetic component of the religious experience must be independently examined. If and when an eidetic analysis discerns cognitive components in the religious act, then the theory of cognitive pluralism will substantiate the claim of religion to theoretical interpretation. However, as long as the cognitive component remains undiscovered, any attempt to justify religious knowledge is futile.

The modern philosophy of religion has found an affirmative answer to the *quid facti* question in the theory of intentionality. The theory of intentionality states that every psychical act is intentional in its character. By intentionality we understand an act coordinated with an object. The intentionality of the logical act—the judgment—was already known to Aristotle. According to his existential theory of the judgment, every logical act predicates either the existence or the non-existence of the object with which it is correlated. But what about other psychical acts, such as the affective and the volitional? Are they likewise intentional, coordinated with an object, or do they move in an ontological vacuum? Classical philosophy never seriously investigated this problem and was inclined rather to deny to these acts the character of intentionality. Of course, the intellectualistic school, regarding the emotional and volitional activities as *modi cogitandi*, had to admit some relationship between them and an objective sphere. Owing, however, to the contempt that philosophers and psychologists alike had for the emotional act (which they considered an *idea confusa*—distorted intellectualistic ideas), they never elaborated the intellectualistic thesis of intentionality. Modern philosophy, although not subscribing to rationalistic dogmas, has, nevertheless, accepted almost as a postulate the intentional character of the psychical act. No psychical act can be performed without coordinating it with an object; the existence, or subsistence or pseudo-reality (Meinong) of an object is warranted by the act itself.

The conclusions which were derived from this theory caused a complete reversal of the traditional attitude towards the affective and volitional experiences. Classical epistemology had viewed them as inferior to logical judgments and never admitted them to the theoretical domain. Modern anti-intellectualistic epistemology and metaphysics as conceived by Rousseau (feeling), Schopenhauer (will), and Schelling (intuition), and developed by Royce, Krueger, Volkelt, Maier and Scheler, seized upon Pascal's *Logique du Coeur*. It declared the existence of a functional, cognitive component in all psychical acts,[48] regardless of whether the genesis of the emotional life be the intellect (Herbart's intellectualistic theory), will (Wundt, Ribot, Lipps' voluntaristic theory), or sensory experience (Lange-

James' physiological theory). Thus the noetic background of the complex mental life has been recognized.[49]

Following in Lotze's footsteps, epistemology analyzes the psychical act in the following manner. First, every psychical act is intentional, coordinated with an object which exists or subsists for the subject. This coordination is synonymous with the act of predication which lends "reality" to the object. I love something real (to me); I hate something real (to me); I fear something real (to me). This "something" is not an illusion or a *fata morgana*, but a "real" object associated with the mental act. Second, in addition to predication, we may discern another function in the psychical act —valuation. Between predication and the final consummation, the subject appraises the object as to its worthiness of the specific act about to be performed.[50]

In sum, we may discern three strata in every intentional act:

    I. The purely logical function (predication);
   II. The act of appraising (valuation);
  III. The final act of love, hate, etc. (consummation of the act).

This means that every intentional act is implicitly a cognitive one.[51] Knowledge of the object is anterior to the affective or volitional performance; without the cognitive apprehension of the object the psychical act would be impossible.[52]

By way of simple illustration,[53] the statement, "I love my country," may be broken into three components:

    I. There exists a country—predication;
   II. This object is worthy of my love—valuation;
  III. I love my country—consummation of the act.

Thus we have the answer to our original problem: Are logical functions and cognitive components to be discerned in the religious act? The religious act is psychical and hence intentional. It is coordinated with an object which the *homo religiosus* must interpret and appraise before suiting it to his specific religious needs. Knowledge is the prerequisite of any psychical act,[54] however simple. It is manifest, therefore, that the religious act, with its intricate structure and all-enveloping character, contains intrinsic cognitive components.

The *homo religiosus*, therefore, is not the naive believer who, when confronted with reality, turns to mysticism and non-rationality. He substitutes neither belief for knowledge nor faith for critical reasoning; no less than the philosopher himself, he is an enthusiastic practitioner of the cognitive act.[55] He comprehends the world from an unique aspect,[56] but this does not devaluate the importance of his cognition.

In stating the case of religious *noesis*, modern philosophy displayed great ingenuity. However, when the barriers separating the *homo religiosus* from the theoretical realm were removed and the path to a new religious perspective lay open, philosophy undid its work. Instead of entrusting religion with exploring the "here and now" reality, it assigned to it the grasping of the ontological and axiological mystery. This was promoted by two leading schools: Ritschlian-Kantian[57] postulate philosophy which duplicated reality, relegating the phenomenal to the scientist and the ontologico-axiological to the theologian; and faith Realism which proclaimed that both the scientist and *homo-religiosus* are concerned with the same appearance of reality and that the latter explores the unconditioned grounds of scientific thought,[58] thus completing the cognitive act of the scientist. Both schools divorced religious knowledge from temporality and sensibility, and referred it to the domain of the Absolute.

The central theme of the religious experience, however, is not the Absolute, but the immediate and phenomenal reality in all its variegated manifestation. Universal knowledge of the Absolute is possible only after the "world of shadows" has been thoroughly explored. In order to find *the* ultimate grounds, religion must begin with the sensible world; otherwise its quest for the transcendental is futile. Man bound fast to temporality, is incapable of tearing himself loose from the moorings of his sensuous environment. He beholds infinity and eternity as reflected in finitude and evanescence. If the categorical outfit of the religious person is borrowed from the scientist's laboratory, the *homo religiosus* can no better penetrate into the realm of the Absolute than the scientist. Availing itself of the conceptual instruments of science, religion cannot hope to succeed where science has failed. The path to the Absolute leads through concrete reality. If religion is not primarily guided by an autonomous method, it will never reach its objective.[59]

The prime problem of the philosophy of religion is not theosophy or theology but the understanding of the sensible world. The *homo religiosus* is not only theocentric but also ontocentric. He is not concerned with interpreting God in terms of the world but the world under the aspect of God. The nonsensical undertaking of applying concepts derived from temporality to eternity was clearly recognized by negative theology which forbade man to reconnoiter in the realm of the essential attributes and limited him to the one of the actional. In doing this, it clearly stated the case of religious noesis and its object. The latter is not a transcendental Divinity, but the immediate reality. The actional attributes, accessible to man's reason, do not lead him directly to a cognition of God, but to cognition of His world.[60] "The heavens declare the glory of God; and the firmament showeth his handiwork (*Psalms* 19:2)."

The aboriginal religious experience, whether related to God in or beyond the world, always conceives Him from the purview of His relation to reality. The white light of divinity is always refracted through reality's "dome of many-coloured glass." No worshipper has ever isolated the idea of God from the concrete world, and placed it in some immaculate transcendental sphere. The religious experience is a composite phenomenon involving not only God but the ego and the sensuous environment of the *homo religiosus*. He seeks direct contact and close companionship with God and perceives Him not in a transcendent glory, alien and sometimes hostile to the world, but in His full proximity and immanence. He views God from the aspect of His creation; and the first response to such an idea is a purified desire to penetrate the mystery of phenomenal reality.[61] The cognition of this world is of the innermost essence of the religious experience.[62]

## II

THE philosophy of religion, if it is earnest in its leanings towards religious noesis, must develop a specific epistemology. Such a discipline would examine basic concepts and forms of reality and fit them into the religious frame. Should this task be undertaken, it would be discovered that many concepts employed by science and philosophy are incompatible with religious theoretical schemes. Elementary concepts such as time, substance, causality and reality, in order to become eligible for religious knowledge, must be reviewed and reinterpreted. In formulating his outlook, the religious person could then avail himself of conceptual apparata reshaped to his cognitive needs.

The category of time may serve as an illustration. The natural sciences attempt to convert time into quantitative chronometry (Bergson) or chronogeography (Russell); the humanistic sciences conceive it as a creative quality identifiable with the stream of consciousness (James) or pure duration (Bergson). Yet, religion can operate neither with the time concept of the physicist nor that of the psychologist. Time for religion is neither a system of reference nor a bed for the stream of mental life, but appears under the guise of a substance bearing accidents. Time is not a mere void but a "reality." Religion ascribes to time attributes such as "holy," "profane," but these can be applied only to a substance. New time vistas must open for the *homo religiosus*.

There is the problem of duality of time and eternity, time and time-endlessness (which is different from eternity). Again, there is the question of God in His full transcendence beyond time, and God in His immanence in time. This problem does not only bear upon the idea of God but also upon the concept of time. God in the temporal world presents the composite of time and eternity; it implies the intrusion of eternity upon temporality. (The clarification of this problem is of the utmost importance to an analysis of the idea of Revelation.)

In this connection, the problem of the calendar bears some investigation. The division of time into days, weeks, months and years is quite incongruous with the time concept of the scientist for whom time is a continuum with no milestone.[63] The seasons of the year or the astronomic phenomena of sunrise and sunset do not, in the least, determine the character of time. On the contrary, like other phenomena they occur *in* time. The religious type, in his experience of this category, identifies the incessant flux of the chronos with the artificial form of the calendar. Even with reference to God, the worshipper ecstatically exclaims "For a thousand years in thy sight are but as a yesterday when it has passed, and as a watch in the night."* He sees God not only in eternity but also in time quantified and measured by the calendar.

The specific religious apprehension of time as cyclic motion or as an eternal repetition (Kierkegaard) is likewise utterly unintelligible to the scientist who measures spatialized time or to the metaphysician who views time as a directed flow. The experience of time as repetition is rooted in the typically religious time-awareness and is closely associated with the concept of the calendar that is indeed pure repetition. The day, the month and the year recur again and again. No organized religion can dispense with such a notion of time; it is irreplaceable for the practical worshipper.

The cyclic appearance of time in religion goes hand in hand with time reversibility. Here again we encounter a notion which is alien to the scientific world-perspective. The scientist can apprehend either a mapped out and retraceable time or a directed time stream which is identical with irrevocable change. If he operates with static, spatialized and reversible time then "becoming" is precluded, as indicated above; for a universe that can retrace its course

*כי אלף שנים בעיניך כיום אתמול כי יעבר ואשמורה בלילה.
(תהלים צ:ד)

and regress in the minus direction with the same ease (theoretically) as it progresses in the plus direction is not susceptible to change. It can always undo the cosmic occurrence of the past. On the other hand, time flow which is continuous becoming renders reversibility impossible for change denotes a movement of superseding phases which cannot be reversed. Yet, the religious time awareness is so paradoxical as to register both becoming *and* reversibility. As to becoming, the idea of Creation introduces it metaphysically; and the religious norm with its associate postulate of freedom sponsors it ethically. Nevertheless, the reversibility of time and of the causal order is fundamental in religion, for otherwise the principle of conversion would be sheer nonsense. The act of reconstructing past psychical life, of changing the arrow of time from a forward to a retrospective direction, is the main premise of penitence. One must admit with Kierkegaard that repetition is a basic religious category. The *homo religiosus,* oscillating between sin and remorse, flight from and return to God, frequently explores not only the traces of a bygone past retained in memory, but a living "past" which is consummated in his emergent time-consciousness.[64] It is irrelevant whether reversibility is a transcendental act bordering upon the miraculous, as Kierkegaard wants us to believe, or a natural phenomenon that has its roots in the unique structure of the religious act. The paradox of a directed yet reversible time concept remains. Neither physicalism nor psychologism throws any light upon a dichotomy which can be understood only against the typical religious cognitive background.

It must be understood that these time concepts are not mere fantasy. They are inherent in the religious consciousness which apprehends time in its own fashion. The structure of such concepts must be investigated. Whether the scientist will agree with such a mode of comprehension is hardly pertinent to the philosopher of religion.

In a similar manner, all basic concepts of reality should be subjected to reexamination. Causality, space, quantity, quality, necessity, etc., will then assume new meaning. If, for example, causality be analysed, it would be seen that neither the mechanistic causality of science nor the sensate, teleological causation of the humanistic sciences suffice for religion. Provocative aspects concerning old problems such as causality and providence, causality and freedom (which is a philosophical, ethical and religious problem), causality and conversion, etc., will then emerge.

Our mode of thinking has so long been shaped by scientific methodology that we can little imagine such an undertaking. From sheer force of habit, the moment we cope with a religious problem we forget its specific structure and we translate "transcendental" viewpoints in terms of scientific and metaphysical concepts. Such methodological confusion dooms any elaboration of the unique religious aspect. The net result is that, instead of rediscovering the typically religious in the noetical field, we move in a vicious circle of rationalization.

III

THE cognitive character of the religious experience having been established, the problem of methodology arises. The unique religious approach to reality needs now to be elaborated. How are we to proceed with the construction of a specific methodology without being handicapped by positivistic and naturalistic philosophical conceptions, on the one hand, and recondite mysticism, on the other?

A simple analysis of the subjective religious experience will not yield the desired objectives. Religious experience, the most elusive and intricate of the mental processes, must be approached with caution. We may be apt to believe that the omniscient "independent" philosopher who has attained almost "infinite" wisdom and acquired the magical faculty of intuiting the pure essences will show the way. As a matter of fact, many enthusiastic philosophers and students of religion have but recently started out on this adventuresome road. Following the footsteps of phenomenological zealots, they have attempted to apprehend the religious experience through a hypersensible act of intuition which is tantamount to a frank admission of defeat for reason. It indicates that the "public" critical reason has been renounced for the sake of a "private" distorted subjective experience. While intuitive thinking for the traditional logician is identical with the aboriginal cognitive flashes of reason which are the antecedents of discursive thinking, modern intuitionism is nothing but pure emotionalism. The autonomous philosophical apprehension of reality is anti-intellectualistic and hostile to critical thinking. It is pretentious and arrogant. It claims to transcend the boundaries of relational scientific knowledge and to reach into the sphere of super-noesis. There, it maintains, reality is revealed intimately to the daring mind; subject and object, mind and absolute Being, merge. It is self-evident that this philosophical temperament is a typical reaction to both positivistic skepticism and naturalistic cognitive monotony. The metaphysical spirit, too long imprisoned in scientific homogeneity, tore itself loose from rational principles and fled the domain of criticism. Pascal's *ordre du coeur, logique de coeur, le coeur a ses raisons*, rediscovered by Scheler and Hartmann, became the central thesis of the de-intellectualized philosophy. If reason is incapable of acquiring intimate knowledge of reality, then, said they, let the heart accomplish this, lest we wander forever in the labyrinths of scientific symbols and substitutes.

To appraise the methodological procedure of modern metaphysics, a double criterion—one practical and the other theoretical—should be applied.

*The practical.* Regardless of the shortcomings of pragmatism as a solution to our most perplexing epistemological problems, it is nevertheless advisable to apply, at times, the pragmatic principle to the appraisal of certain philosophical theories. Epistemology would do well to cast aside such canonized concepts as objectivity and ethical neutrality and survey philosophical doctrines from a subjective, normative viewpoint. The ethical implications of any philosophical theory, as to its beneficence or detriment to the moral advancement of man, should many a time decide the worth of the doctrine. A philosophical ideology should be measred not only by purely theoretical standards but by ethical ones as well. Now let us examine the aftermath of epistemological anti-intellectualism rampant in European philosophy during much of this century. What were the consequences of the romantic escape of the theoretical man, fleeing from the serene realm of rational knowledge into the wilderness of intuitionism? A study of the forces which shaped contemporary European culture gives ample

instance of the dangers germane to subjective intuitive
attitudes. Autonomous metaphysics, deserting reason,
often leads to moral corruption.[65]

There is little distinction between the medieval mysticism
of Meister Eckhardt and Jakob Boehme and that of contemporary emotionalism embellished in philosophical ver-
biage. Both display a definite trend to deliver philosophical
thinking from the yoke of reason. Mystical trends which
dominated Bergson's biologism and intuitionism, phenomenological emotionalism, the so-called humanistic hermeneutics, and the modern existential philosophy have
played a prominent role in the confusion that pervaded
European thought. It is no mere coincidence that the most
celebrated philosophers of the third Reich were outstanding disciples of Husserl. Husserl's intuitionism (*Wesensschau*)
which Husserl, a trained mathematician, strived to keep
on the level of mathematical intuition, was transposed into
emotional approaches to reality. When reason surrenders
its supremacy to dark, equivocal emotions, no dam is able
to stem the rising tide of the affective stream.

The modern philosopher-mystic is a disguised apostle
of Dionysus (Nietzsche's life-affirming God). Both see their
antagonist in the logical Socrates, the inventor of the class
concept and the crusader for an intellectualistic morality.
Dionysian mystic wisdom versus "decadent" Socratism was
the philosophical Armaggedon of our age. "The society
of life-affirmers" whose task was the reestablishment of
"superabundance of life," brought havoc and death
instead. They left in their wake "*Wahn, Wille, Wehe*", and
the "rebirth of tragedy."[66]

All the racial theories so prominent during this century
have evolved from the modern concept of "wholeness."
The latter has become the touchstone of modern philoso-

phy and so-called *Weltanschauungslehre*. The scientific concept of Gestalt was transformed into something mythical and the idea of the structure into mystical Dionysian knowledge of "Primal Unity."

The new Gestalt approach, well-founded in contemporary scientific thought, was applied not only to the psyche, but also to the psycho-physical ego, both individual and collective. Modern philosophical anthropology endeavors to grasp the whole structure of man, both the corporeal and psychical man, as a morphological problem. In such fashion it has attempted to interrelate human behavior with physiognomic characteristics (Kretsmcher, Klages, Utitz). All this perhaps is pregnant with new ideas capable of enriching our knowledge of man and his destiny. The impartial theoretician, however, must constantly be circumspect of the Janus-face of the Gestalt approach; for it may become pseudo-scientific and recrudescence into moral corruption. Such scientific laxity actually did atrophy European culture in the period following World War I. No concept ever degenerated to such a degree and became so powerful a weapon in the hands of fanatics as did the Gestalt. An untrammeled path led from Gestalt and group psychology through typology, philosophical anthropology and characterology (in conjunction with graphology and physiognomics)[67] into the welter of racial theory. It appears that the "good old" atomistic method is less vulnerable to misapplication than the new humanistic and philosophical hermeneutics which require constant vigilance.

In particular is this true of philosophical religion where subjectivistic gods have reigned since the days of Schleiermacher and Kierkegaard. Here mysticism celebrated its greatest triumph. Meister Eckhardt was proclaimed the philosopher. His non-given God, "the still desert" (*die stille Wueste*) replaced the God of revelation.

It need hardly be stressed that this reduction of religion into some recondite, subjective current is absolutely perilous. It frees every dark passion and every animal impulse in man. Indeed, it is of greater urgency for religion to cultivate objectivity than perhaps for any other branch of human culture. If God is not the source of the most objectified norm, faith in Him is nothing but an empty phrase. Pluralism by no means indicates escapism and romanticism in knowledge. If cognitive approaches to reality exist apart from the scientific, then they must be based upon strictly logico-epistemological principles. They cannot be permitted to run amok in a subjective world. It is indeed unfortunate that pluralism, originally well-intended, has, in certain doctrines, assumed proportions that undermine the most elementary principles of reason. To avert misery and confusion the human mind would do well were it to approach the subjective realm with far greater caution and reserve than it has in the past.

*The theoretical.* The chief argument of the philosopher— that the natural sciences, instead of photographing nature, create symbolic equivalents—is, of course, valid as we have seen the physicists themselves admit. But this does not prove that the modern philosopher, in contrast with the scientist, grasps the core of nature by the hypersensible act of placing himself in the "flux." The inability of the physicist to free himself from numerical constructs does not establish his indictment, nor does it apotheosize the metaphysician. The latter, perhaps unconsciously, emulates the scientific method and creates metaphysical symbols, under the illusion of interpreting the ογτως ογ, the "really real." Be that as it may, epistemological pluralism has not abandoned the realm of logic. It says only that reason itself leads the physicist, psychologist, philosopher, and *homo religiosus* to a pluralism of viewpoints. The heterogeneity of knowledge, however, is not based upon a manifold of methods employed by theoreticians, but upon the plurality of the objective orders they encounter.

Let us elaborate this thesis. If we were to scrutinize metaphysical arguments carefully, we would find that many of the new aspects of reality which philosophy and the humanities claim to have discovered are not alien to the natural sciences.[68] Instance the Gestalt[69] concept which was the crucial issue raging between metaphysics and the mathematical sciences. Modern physics knows of and employs the structural approach in its formulation of the physical universe. As a matter of fact, when we trace the history of the modern concept of the whole, we notice a peculiarity, namely, that Gestalt was introduced by a physicist before psychology and modern philosophy had but the vaguest notion of it. In 1873 James Clerk Maxwell wrote that two approaches to reality, both typical of scientific thinking, exist in the mathematical sciences: the piece-meal, which integrates the whole out of its components; and the structural, which proceeds conversely. He further stated that a mathematical method (the partial differential equations and their integrations over a continuous field) might be devised enabling the physicist to proceed from the whole to the parts.[70] This structural approach has become the basic method of quantum and wave mechanics.[71] The latter, which describes aggregates and not individual particles, interprets the physical process in Gestalt terms. The innermost essence of quantum probability lies in its statistical laws which, governing aggregations, are not derived by examining each individual particle (as was the case in the kinetic theory of matter) but are obtained by an immediate approach to the aggregate. The behavior of the individual is determined in a statistical manner by the quantum system.[72] The physical system (the whole) displays properties which cannot be discovered "by dividing it into its component parts," for it is never "equal simply to the sum of its various parts."

The manner in which quantum and wave mechanics operate with the new structural aspects has enormous metaphysical implications. It has definite bearing upon the most basic principles of the physical universe, namely, space, time, causality and motion. As regards causality and motion, the resultant aggregate determined by arbitrary external factors (as described in classical mechanics) is replaced by a whole which implies immanent morphological designs; affecting the concept of motion and causality. "The Eigenfunctions of the atoms and molecules no longer depend upon contingent or arbitrary factors, that are determined by nature. The Eigenfunctions are actually the decisive Gestalt elements of the observable occurrence."[73]

Space and time were "deposed from the dominant position which they held in Newtonian physics and (are) relegated to a status more or less resembling that which they held in the scholastic philosophy. The atom, which has a potency of various states, is correlated to the states as potency is to the act. It endures as the atom, while it takes different states in succession. This is precisely the aspect of things on which Aristotle fixed his attention. That substratum which persists while receiving different determinations is what, in the Aristotelian Scholastic philosophy, is called matter; whereas the structural principle which is peculiar to each determination or state is called form. The atom, then, is matter with respect to its states which are forms."[74]

Thus the complaints of the philosopher, that the physicist is deprived of a "sixth sense" which would enable him to envisage the structural whole, are unjustified. In fact, science considers the whole as the ultimate ground of the physical process, and the philosopher is not the only one who observes the movement of the particles under the aspect of totality. One the one hand, it would appear that the "independent" philosopher is celebrating his greatest victory, for even the physicist bowed to his will and accepts the structural approach. On the other hand, however, the emergence of the new concepts in the natural sciences renders the errors and fallacies of contemporary metaphysics more flagrant. Ostensibly this is a conditional victory, for, while modern physics bears out the Gestalt theory, it refutes the means and methodical schemes employed by modern philosophy. Let us not forget that the whole is of a qualitative nature. Form, both in the Aristotelian and modern sense, denotes the *quale* character of reality. A system-whole, on both microscopic and macroscopic levels, if viewed outside the system, eludes scientific interpretation. The cosmos in its totality, as portrayed by Goethe and Spinoza, can, if viewed from without, never be subject to quantitative measurements and causalistic determination. The scientist operates within, not outside the whole. Causality can never overreach the boundary of the cosmic process. Should we interrogate the physicist as to his description of the concept of nature, he would (perforce) admit that the idea of wholeness is but an empty phrase, not suitable for portraying nature as such. The atomicity of matter and energy, which is still a postulate in physics, gives priority to the atomistic method. The latter is inherent in the quantitative mode of the physical universe. Only component parts can be posited as scientifically explicable.

Now the question arises as to the physicist's arrival at the structural whole which is a qualitative aspect of reality. How did science postulate wholeness and immanence in our universe? Ostensibly it was an act of self-transcendence; science went beyond its own limits. But how did this occur? The only answer to this question is that science apprehended the whole within the system through an act of *reconstruction*. The physical problem of reality still retains its piecemeal character. Antinomies and deformities in the summative appearance of the universe, not in its structural whole, are still the problems of modern physics. The new Gestalt element finds its expression and formulation in mathematical equations that determine the single processes within the system. The single particle is not described by arbitrary external factors but via the system. Structural designs are accessible only insofar as they can be translated into mathematical equations determining the status of the particles. The structural whole itself, if viewed outside the system, remains indefinable and causalistically inexplicable. It merely serves the physicist when operating with the system as a source of information concerning its individual phenomena on the microscopic level. The physicist's interest is limited to the behavior of the particles out of which he methodically reconstructs the whole, which in turn determines the behavior of its "infinitesimal" components.

The scientific universe, then, was shaped in the following manner: First, physics encountered a promiscuous qualitative mass which eluded scientific scrutiny. Second, in order to overcome this obstruct, science constructed its own object by duplicating nature and correlating numerical equivalents with intangible qualitative phenomena. This method is epitomized in atomization and piecemeal summation. (At this point classical mechanics considered its task done.) Third, modern physics, confronted by the enigmatic behavior of certain "strings of events" and not finding an adequate answer in the atomistic method, reversed its procedure and applied a structural aspect. Yet, this new Gestalt element grew out of the former summative method.

The immediate apprehension of the configuration is a sheer myth incompatible with epistemological facts. It is beyond the scope of both the physicist and humanist. The synthetic aggregate is not the shibboleth of physics nor is the primitive whole the birthmark of modern humanities. The understanding of both nature and spirit is dualistic, mosaic and structurl—but (and this is of enormous importance) the mosaic and structural approaches are not two disparate methodological aspects which may be independently pursued: they form one organic whole. First, as we have indicated, the scientist encountering a qualitative flux applies the atomistic yardstick to single component parts. Second, progressing from one plane (macroscopic) to another (microscopic) he reconstructs structural patterns that enable him to describe the behavior of the simple elements which the atomistic method postulated. This new viewpoint, however, cannot be gained without consideration of our piecemeal contact with reality lest it lead to arbitrary extravagances. The humanist must adjust himself to the same procedure if he wishes to avoid excessive philosophical hermeneutics. The only difference between nature and spirit as regards these two methods is that the former lends itself more readily to an atomistic interpretation than the latter. While the physicist, for a time, was able to satisfy his needs with the atomization method, the humanist has long felt the dearth of a new methodological aspect. The physicist considered his mosaic approach quite adequate for the explanation of certain segments of reality (macroscopic), whereas exact quantification and precise formulation seemed a foregone conclusion. The humanist, however, not possessing the instruments of geometrization, and hence unable to cope with single components, was compelled to pursue other patterns. With the emergence of microphysics, the situation underwent a radical change. The piecemeal approach was no longer commensurable with physical facts and both physicist and psychologist turned to the whole. Yet, the quest for new designs can be realized only if guided by objective atomistic criteria.

The modern metaphysician, in contrast with the physicist, does not employ the painstaking method of reconstruction but finds the whole even before he has apprehended the components. As a matter of fact, he denies the existence of the parts. There is nothing but wholeness and totality. The structural, all-embracing totality is not only metaphysically but also methodologically antecedent to the *modi*. While the scientist postulates the whole on atomistic premises—starting from the parts and reconstructing the whole for the purpose of describing the former—the philosopher constructs it forthwith.

In view of this, it would be fallacious to apply the method of independent philosophy in the field of religion. It would inevitably result in a labyrinth of mysticism. If modern philosophy, in its quest for "independence," has become arbitrary, then religious thought, which is particularly prone to abstruseness, needs be all the more wary of such an alignment. The student of religion, starting from the principle of cognitive pluralism, would act wisely in taking his cue from the scientist rather than the philosopher. The structural designs of religion cannot be intuited through any sympathetic fusion with an eternal essence, but must be reconstructed out of objective religious data and central realities. The uniqueness of the religious experience resides in its objective normative components.

## IV

WE may gain access to religious knowledge of reality with its unique structural aspects in a two-fold way: First, by coordinating two series in the religious sphere, the subjective and the objective; and second, by reconstructing the former out of the latter.[75] Let us elaborate this thesis and determine the method that it entails. For the sake of expedience, we shall again refer to the scientist's approach to external reality and, by comparison, understand the specific method which we would do well to pursue in the field of philosophy of religion.

As we have seen, classical mechanics was aware of two orders: the subjective qualitative, obtained through sense experience, and the objective quantitative, postulated by scientific methodology. Modern physics adds a third order, the subjective structural which is reconstructed out of the summative objective. However, both classical and modern physics agree that the primeval subjective "order" is beyond the pale of science. It exists *de facto* without any logical legitimation. The parallelism of these two series does not intrigue the scientist who is not eager to interpret qualitative phenomena. The natural sciences, classical and modern, maintain that even if we are cognizant of a mysterious correlation between these two orders, the qualitative or subjective series can never be explained. Science is interested only in constructing a quantitative correlate which corresponds in an incomprehensible way to sensuous qualitative phenomena. Color or sound is not to be explained by its quantitative counterpart in the objective order. *Quanta* never explain *qualia*. Both are unfolded in different dimensions thus precluding any scientific or metaphysical interpretation. It is only in the quantitative domain that the scientist finds his object. It is there that he searches for order and regularity, for a causal nexus and a systematic sequence. He coordinates the objective and subjective series without ever exploring the qualitative relata. A and B are members of the objective series and B is explained by A. But $A_1$ and $B_1$—elements in the subjective series—remain as isolated phenomena. The scientist can never construct a causal relation between them.

The method applied by the scientist in his interpretation is the so-called explanatory method, which is concerned primarily with the interrelations and interdependencies of successive phases in the objective order. The so-called matter stratum merely serves the physicist as an ideal premise from which he interprets the process. The scientist's interest is absorbed by the "how" question. How does B exist? The scientist asks for the relational necessity of B since, for him, the existence of a phenomenon within the cosmic process is identical with ontic necessity. The mathematical sciences look askance upon existence *de facto* and seek to legitimate existence *de jure*. The law of transient causality is the instrument of the scientist in his endeavor to formulate a principle of necessity within the cosmic process. In contrast with scholastic doctrines, physics identifies ontic necessity with an existence conditioned by an external cause. In order to postulate relational necessity, the scientist attempts to eliminate the contingent character of nature. While existence *de facto* does not require any causal interpretation, existence *de jure* must be causal coordinated. Even in quantum mechanics we have the probability wave function which describes the behavior of a particle within the system. Such a necessary existence can be established only in the objective order. The *quid juris* question cannot be applied to the qualitative universe. In this respect, classical and modern physics agree.

This duality of aspects presents a philosophical problem which was the crucial issue between Kantianism and Neo-Kantianism. The controversy revolved around the emergence of knowledge, or the "movement of the logos." How does knowledge proceed? Does the "logos" move from sense experience to a postulated world or conversely? In other words, is subjectivity to be construed in terms of objectivity or vice versa?

Kant assumed that human knowledge is based upon the duality of receptivity and spontaneity. When we encounter the Unknown, two things occur. First, we are struck by something "transcendent" which affects us with its aboriginal force; and second, our reason, utilizing the categorical apparata, moulds this distorted υλη (*hylé*) into definite concepts and ideas. Kant considered the receptive act to be anterior to the spontaneous. Sensible awareness delivers the sensuous raw material, and reason, as a formative principle, forms it. Experience, seen not only against its genetic psychological background but even against a methodological one, progresses, according to Kant, from qualitative sensation to scientific thinking.

At this point, Neo-Kantians, guided by panlogistic Hegelian tendencies, departed from their master and reversed the entire procedure. Experience, according to the Neo-Kantians (Marburg School), instead of passing onward from subjectivity to objectivity, gravitates in the opposite direction, from postulated "ideal" magnitudes to its emergence in the form of "concrete reality" (*Wirklichkeit*). The main philosophical feat of a the Neo-Kantians consisted of the elimination of the receptive components of experience. They contended that even the so-called qualitative data are nothing but the product of a spontaneous mental act. Pure experience, stripped of all spontaneous additions and reduced to given primordial elements is, despite positivistic contentions, non-existent. There is no given sensation, just as there is no given thinking. Hence, the Neo-Kantian school further maintained that it is absolutely fallacious to state that experience proceeds from the qualitative to the quantitative, from the subjective to the objective. On the contrary, it is the objective sphere that makes it possible for subjective "data" to spring into being. The sensation of color always appears on the canvas of space and time. The space and time coordinates do not present the frame of receptivity, as Kant thought, but are spontaneous creations of pure thinking.[76] Any sensational apprehension is conditioned by its antecedent, the act of creative objectification. Whatever the argument, the Neo-Kantian school reversed the procedure and envisaged experience as moving from the objective to the subjective order. Only by reversing the objective order may the subjective background be apprehended.

It is to be emphasized that the whole controversy concerning the priority of the subjective and objective spheres is of theoretical value only. It is an epistemological problem regarding the method to which the philosopher needs recourse in his attempt to reconstruct the process of noetical experience. In practice, however, subjective data can never be used as a starting point, for, just as there is no ideal objectivity, there is also no pure subjectivity. If positivistic philosophy speaks of isolating given elements from additional spontaneous constructs within the complex of experience, the thesis has meaning only in the sense of *re*construction. We do not find two different components, the subjectively given and the objectively constructed, but one unified phenomenon. And the isolation of its components can be affected only by the method of reconstruction.

Even were we to admit, with the positivists, that a sensuous substratum persists after the elimination of all conceptual addenda, we must nonetheless begin with the objectified phenomena in order to obtain the pure sensible quality. The positivists, speaking of an adequate sensuous experience undisturbed by the interference of our reason, cannot demonstrate their thesis with an immediate approach to primitive sensibility. They must resort to objectified perceptual contents and by the method of reconstruction strip our experience of all objective elements like time, space, intensity, quality, etc. The entire controversy loses its importance if it is viewed from a practical methodical viewpoint.

The above mentioned dual character of reality is applicable not only to the external, but also to the internal world. There is a dualism of objectivity and subjectivity in the manifestation of the spirit. The process of objectification is not limited to that reality enveloped by space and time, but extends to the one embraced by time and consciousness. Whenever we speak of spiritual phenomena, we already have in mind objectified phenomena. Needless to state, this process of objectification is not as complete and ideal in the realm of the spirit as it is in nature. The method of quantification cannot be applied to spiritual manifestations since they lack extension, which is a prerequisite for quantification. In the external world, time itself is quantified by projection on a spatial background. In the internal world, however, where time is never reflected in a spatial mirror, exact quantification is impossible. (This was overlooked by Fechner, the father of psychophysics, who attempted to measure mental processes in a manner similar to that of the physicist in the world of dynamics.) Nevertheless, there is a process of objectification, however imperfect, in the realm of inwardness. Thus, ethical subjectivity is converted into propositions, norms, values, etc.,[77] which are nothing but objectified correlates of an elusive subjective stream. In the aesthetic sphere, subjectivity finds expression either in the discipline of aesthetics or in works of art. Both are objectified aspects of ephemeral subjectivity. Religion, which is perhaps more deeply rooted in subjectivity than any other manifestation of the spirit, is also reflected in externalized phenomena which are evolved in the objectification process of the religious consciousness. The aggregate of religious objective constructs is comprised of ethico-religious norms, ritual, dogmas, theoretical postulates, etc.

There is a definite trend towards self-transcendence on the part of the spirit.[78] It strives to escape its private inwardness and infiltrate the concrete world encompassed by space and pervaded by corporeal forms. The morphological process of self-realization from the inward to the outward is typical of the spiritual act. The arrow points towards externality, spatialization and quantification; and subjectivity rushes along this route. Of course, the lack of easily manipulated quantifying instruments is a tremendous handicap. Nevertheless, the spirit tirelessly endeavors to achieve an end which lies beyond its limits and ends. It objectifies itself in the emergence of a certain order which in turn finds its correlate in space and time extension. The objectifying process consists of two incongruous parts. The first remains within the world where subjective and objective aspects are rooted in pure qualitative strata, differing only as to their degree of distinctness and as to their proximity to the psychophysical border. The second is an act of emergence of "spiritual" reality into outward tangible forms. This concrete physical order, enveloped by time and space, is coordinated with its correlate in the internal world. The internal subjective correlate is, in turn, the objectified expression of some more primitive subjectivity. Religious subjectivity, for example, finds its correlate in a certain norm which, though remaining within spiritual bounds, strives towards the mysterious junction of *psyche* and *physis*. The norm is much nearer to the outer fringes of externality than its counterpart, the quasi–non-normative subjectivity. The norm, in such a semi-objectified state, attempts to break through the barrier separating the physical from the spiritual in order to appear in the arena of life. The consummation of the religious act always takes place in a non-personal world.

To illustrate, we may analyze the triad in the God-man relation: first, the subjective, private finitude-infinity tension; second, the objective normative outlook; and third, the full, concrete realization in external and psychophysical acts. A subjective God-man relation implies various contradictory states. These are wrath and love, remoteness and immanence, repulsion and fascination (on the part of divinity), tremor and serenity, depression and rapture, flight and return (on the part of man), etc.[79] This subjective attitude in man is in turn reflected either in the form of logico-cognitive judgments or in ethico-religious norms, e.g., God exists; He is omniscient; He is omnipresent; He is omnipotent; He is merciful; He is vengeful; He is the Creator, etc. You shall love God; you shall fear Him; you shall worship Him; you shall love your fellowman, etc. These judgments and norms lying in the immediate proximity of the psychophysical threshold tend to externalize themselves. They find their concrete expression in articles of faith, in prayers, in physical acts of worship, and in other practices and observances, all of which lie in the external world. Ostensibly, religion, though flowing in the deepest subliminal ego-strata, is in eternal quest for spatialization and corporeal manifestation.

What is more, comparative studies in the field of religion have ascertained that of the two methods of objectification, the ethos and the cult, the latter is more typical of the unique religious experience. In its attempt to freeze subjective religiosity into solid and stable forms, religion prefers the cult to the ethos. Whenever religion exploits the moral consciousness—the ethical "ought"—for its own needs and ends, we must discriminate between the objective form delivered by the ethos and the unique, subjective religious content. The imperatives, "Thou shalt not murder," "Thou shalt help thy fellowman," "Thou shalt not perjure," though included in any system of secular ethics, are nevertheless specific religious commandments. Yet, when religious subjectivity is crystallized into forms of ritual, the subjective and objective lie within the framework of the religious consciousness.

Religion is always typified and described not so much

by its ethos as by its ritual and cult. The existence of an ethical norm is a common denominator in all religious systems. The unique character of a particular religion, however, appears only in the ritual. Positive religion must always be measured by the yardstick of ritualism, not by that of the ethos. This does not mean that religion can, in any way, dispense with the ethos. Far from it. Both ritual and ethos inhere in the religious act. The cancellation of morality in religion would render it synonymous with barbarity and paganism. The dissociation of the religious act from its non-rational worship and ritual is identical with the resolution of the religious experience into a secular morality and a mundane ethical culture. The superiority of the ritual is to be understood only from the viewpoint of religious typology which treats of the unique in religion.

The triple relation of the subjective, objective and concrete in the religious sphere characterizes all manifestations of the spirit in ethics, aesthetics, etc. The ethical person does not only tend to mould a clear norm with his subjective duty-consciousness, but to realize this norm in concrete life. One of the weak points of Kantian ethics is that it does not provide consistently for the externalization of inwardness. The decision is the final act of the free will, the agent of the ethical process. Kant's ethics offer no approach to the consummation of the decision. The realization of the summun bonun does not depend upon the free will, but is conditioned by faith.[80]

As heretofore indicated, both classical and modern physics ignored the primordial subjective "order" we encounter. Scientific cognition is essentially the establishment of interdependencies among the phases of the objective order. Classical and modern physics differ only in their relation to a third reconstructed qualitative structural order. While the mechanist of old was content with the summative objective series, his modern successor reconstructs "subjective" structural aspects. In this regard, it has been emphasized that humanistic sciences and religion should follow in the footsteps of modern physics and reconstruct subjective aspects out of the objective order. The main shortcoming of the naturalistic school was not so much the postulate of methodological uniformity in regard to nature and spirit as the delimiting of knowledge to the piecemeal interpretation of the objective order. As long as physics operated with a single atomistic approach, its method could not benefit the humanistic sciences, which can ill afford to ignore the subjective aspect. The inversion of the objective into the subjective is a fundamental method of the humanist. However, as soon as the modern physicist had evolved a "subjective" cosmos-whole out of the "objective" summative universe, the humanist found his mentor: in the humanistic field any objective relational construct must be coordinated with its coefficient in the subjective sphere; while causality in nature may be exclusively restricted to objective numerical equivalents, the corresponding concept in spiritual reality must be studied against its subjective background.

As we have seen, when the scientist states that A is the cause of B, he is unconcerned with the subjective correlates $A_1$ and $B_1$. No reference to the primordial subjective part of reality is necessary for the construction of a causal vinculum. A causal nexus between quantitative phenomena does not imply a parallel relation between their qualitative counterparts. The latter escapes the scientists measuring rods.

And yet in contrast with this, it is impossible to construct a causal bond in objectified spiritual reality without recourse to its subjective correlate. When we speak, for instance, of causality in the realm of religion, we cannot say that A (a certain religious norm) is the cause of B, since there is no direct contact between A and B. A and B are not autonomous phenomena but rather the end-products of a long process of objectification. Any kind of relational postulation between the end-products of the series must begin with subjective phases of the process. Comparative religion does not explain objective positive religious data by establishing abstract general interdependencies between them, but reconstructs the subjective aspect of religiosity and traces causation to that medium. In effect, whereas classical science performs an act of construction to determine causality, philosophy of religion performs an act of reconstruction. However, through reconstruction, the principle of causality assumes new and modified significance. The relationship of cause and effect, with reference to the conservation of energy, fundamental in classical physics, is not veridical in the realm of the spirit, since the equality can be established only if causality be restricted to objective data. We measure A and B and we compare them. However, if A and B are not directly coordinated and must be reconverted first into their subjective aspects $A_1$ and $B_1$, then it is apparent that such a relationship is non-existent. It is a well known fact in modern psychology that insignificant incidents sometimes give rise to changes and transformations of cataclysmic proportions, whereas events of the utmost importance frequently fail to impress the human mind and fade into complete oblivion.

What we see then is the following: Any objective series in the field of religion can neither be understood nor explained on its own merit. The subjective track must be explored,[81] for sometimes identical objective constructs may represent antipodal subjective aspects. The historian of religion, engaged in comparative studies, is powerless to interpret his data unless he traces a positive set of beliefs, dogmas, norms and customs to the subjective sphere. Any comparison of objectified norms, without the perspective of subjectivity, is totally misfounded.

This thesis can be illustrated by a concrete example drawn from the history of philosophy. We are wont to speak of a causal relation existing between Maimonides and Thomas Aquinas. But what is understood by that causal bond? Our first reaction is that some correlation exists between Maimonides' *Guide of the Perplexed* and Thomas' *Summa Theologica*. But it is nonsensical to speak of a causal nexus existing between two books. Therefore, out of the concrete "Guide" and "Summa" two theological systems are reconstructed. This again does not solve our problem, for it is inconceivable that a causal relation exist between two philosophical systems. The act of reconstruction continues. Out of these systems, methodological reasoning is brought into focus. Philosophical temperaments come to the fore. Our exploration of the subjective route does not stop with this phase but proceeds to penetrate further into the complicated and mysterious sphere of subjectivity. Through the individual subjective philosophizing the clandestine ego emerges from its involuted and ramified recesses. We delve persistently into the enigmatic, subjective mists. Yet, however far the regressive movement continues, we are never quite able to fathom subjectivity. What we call subjectivity is only a surface reproduction which still needs exploration. An infinite regression takes place along the stationary track left behind the objectifying "logos." The destination is always at an infinite distance. In contrast with the physicist whose quest, regardless of the structural aspects prevalent in modern science, is for progressive objectification, the humanist strives for ever regressing "subjectification." In both cases, causation is not final but continues to move with the scientist in a "plus" direction (from the concrete macroscopic to the symbolic microscopic level) and with the humanist in a "minus" direction. It is therefore impossible to discover final causation in the spiritual realm. Any subjective[82] stage to which we may point with satisfaction can never be considered ultimate. We may always proceed further and discover yet a deeper stratum of subjectivity.

If the introduction of subjective aspects requires an act of retrospection, even as regards the physical universe, then it is all the more necessary in the realm of the spirit. The starting point in any analysis of subjectivity must be the objective order. It is impossible to gain any insight into the subjective stream unless we have previously acquired objective aspects.[83]

V

THIS viewpoint is demonstrable in any field of the spiritual sciences. The analysis of a work of art or an ethical maxim is synonymous with the act of retracing the route along which objectifying creativity moves. Eliminate the objective criteria, however, and entrance to the enchanted sphere of subjectivity is immediately barred. Were we, for instance, to analyze Plato's philosophy, we would reconstruct the subjective aspects of his creativity such as the compenetration of environment and individual psyche, the convergence of society and the aloofness of the genius, the conflux of universal cultural forces, and the uniqueness of character, etc. The key to all these subjective phenomena lies hidden in Plato's metaphysics, physics, and psychology which are elaborated in the printed pages of his works. The historian exhumes a long vanished world out of calligraphic symbols. This is nothing but the restoration of the objectified form to its contextual subjectivity; this is an act of reconstruction. However, no magician, given the same subjective data, could predict the objective patterns of Plato's philosophy. No sojourner in the land of subjectivity can determine antecedently the phases of the objectifying process. The emergence of the inward into the outward, of the subjective into the objective, can never be divined, since the "logos" itself—the process of cognition and the approach to the transcendent object—must of necessity remain inscrutable.

However, if the correlative nature of subjectivity and objectivity are to be described, the following thesis must be posited. Both are "real" and both lie within the ontic realm. Their only distinguishing feature is that, while objectivity is constructed by an incomprehensible act of the "logos" and is methodologically prior to the subjective aspect, subjectivity is reconstructed by an epistemological act. Subjectivity cannot be approached directly; it must first be objectified by the "logos."

Aristotle's metaphysics instances an outstanding illustration of the reconstruction method. The ontological hierarchy of matter and form, beginning with primordial matter and ending with pure form, suggests a duality similar to that of objectivity and subjectivity. It is known that Aristotle, who in this respect followed his master Plato, considered matter beyond the reach of knowledge. For him the particular and accidental (matter) could never be subordinated to the act of cognition, which was limited to the universal and essential (the form). Nevertheless Aristotle spoke of matter, and his entire philosophy is indeed based upon the polarity of matter and form. Yet, how could he have arrived at the concept of matter, if it be an incomprehensible one? The answer is that he applied the method of reconstruction. By a retrospective analysis of forms, starting from the higher and traveling in the direction of the lower, he came upon the existence of matter. We know that in the Aristotelian hierarchy pure matter is a fiction. Matter exists only after it has been actualized by the concept. This actualization again serves as a new potential out of which a higher degree of morphological realization may emerge. Matter and form (with the exception of pure matter which is non-existent and pure form which is identical with God) are not two disparate realms, but represent different methodological arrows that determine the movement of *noesis*. Whatever is matter for the upward phase is at the same time form for the downward phase. The starting point in Aristotelian philosophy has always been form and never matter. For this reason Aristotle eliminated the possibility of pure matter, since the latter could never be reconstructed from pure form. Form itself, which served him as the ideal Being identical with regularity and lawful existence, is objectivity. Matter is to be conceived as a chaotic, lawless, and unregulated welter which is akin to the modern concept of transient subjectivity. Modern philosophy differs from the Aristotelian only in that it ascribes full ontological value to subjectivity. Contemporary epistemology has no ontological hierarchy and considers the distinction between subjectivity and objectivity to be only directional.

In other fields of philosophical endeavor, philosophers practiced caution in their venture to unify reality and eliminate its dual character *volens nolens* they sifted volatile subjective aspects through the sieve of objective verification. Both the most fanatic of positivists and the most zealous of idealists were compelled to reckon with objective cognitive standards. In the religious domain, however, philosophers often abolished all rules of objectivity. Not only did modern psychologists (who in subtlety and casuistry of speculation surpass the most daring of metaphysicians) sin against religious common sense and indisputable fact, but even philosophers, preachers and religious enthusiasts distorted axiomatic religious truths. Religious subjectivism was born out of the matrix of faith philosophy (Pascal, Rousseau, Hamann, Herder) which traced religious verities to emotional sources. Schleiermacher, Kierkegaard, Wilhelm Hermann, Auguste Sabatier and others were among the consecrated priests who worshipped God in the temples of inwardness and mental craving. It is irrelevant whether the desire to equate the religious act with the inward experience stems from romantic and pietistic sources (Schleiermacher) or from Hegelian doctrines (Kierkegaard) which supplant the ontological *factum* with *fieri* and the *actum* with *actus*; or from Ritschlian views (Wilhelm Hermann) that identify the religious act with the apprehension and appreciation of values. What is important, however, is the fact that the subjectivistic school intrigued many great minds who, sundered by the colliding forces of faith and knowledge, hoped to find quiescence in subjectivism. In freeing religion from any association with an objective performance, be it either theoretical or practical, they hoped to turn religion into an impregnable fortress.[84] If the latter is "neither knowledge nor action but an immedi-

ate consciousness of an all-engulfing feeling of depend-
ence,"[85] then it is impervious to scientific or ethical ambus-
cade. If faith "protests every form of objectivity and it
desires that the subject should be infinitely concerned
about himself without coming into any contact with the
'world-historical',"[86] then there is no common meeting
ground for religion and mundane culture.

The maintenance of the subjectivistic doctrine presents
three problems.[87]

*First, although it is simple enough for the philosopher to speak of
religious subjectivism, it is almost impossible for a representative of a
theistic, apocalyptic religion to satisfy his needs with mere inward
religiosity.* To illustrate this, let us consider the starting points
of philosophical and revealed religion. The philosopher, an
adherent of *religio naturalis*, envisages God as primarily an
infinite ideal to which he aspires. His philosophical religiosity is anthropocentric and anthropocratic. The point of
departure is not God but the inward experience (of Him),
which is considered creative, redeeming and inspiring—
the maximum bonum of mental life. He is absorbed in his
own self rather than in a transcendent God. The norm, if
such exists in the philosopher's religion, plays a secondary
part. With the demotion of the norm and the elimination of
the practical outlook, subjectivism becomes quite acceptable. Religion then is attenuated into sentimentalism, and
God is arrested within inwardness. In contrast with the
philosopher, the essential problem of the *homo religiosus* (in
this context, the believer in revealed religion) is a normative
one. It is directed at explicit knowledge and concrete action
and not at aboriginal, private "immediate consciousness."
"How should I act in daily life? How should I live according
to the will of God? What are the divine attributes I must

accept?"[88]—these are problems of the *homo religiosus*. Not only does the *homo religiosus* differ from the mundane type in feeling and thinking but also in actions. He sets an adamant face towards an encroaching milieu and strives to change it. He does not live in an isolated refuge of mental solitude nor is he exclusively immersed in his own existence. The accounts so frequently related by the historians of religion concerning the solitary life of the eremites[89] or even of the monastery which flourishes today,[90] are not typical of the modern *homo religiosus*.[91] Apocalyptic religion at the very outset excludes extravagant religious individualism. It is not only the individual ego, even though endowed with supernatural faculties, but the entire community that meets God.[92] Revealed religion rests upon the idea of a charismatic social ego that is the living incarnation of the faith. Biblical narrative concerning the prophets in Israel does not depict them as hermits who severed all intercourse with their fellowmen and fled into the desert of mental seclusion. They were, above all, men of action, dominated by an all-consuming passion for reform and change. Not only did they preach God's word on street corners and in the market place, but they apprehended Him in the welter of the manswarm. Even the supernal drama of revelation was unfolded before the multitude. It would seem that the old Aristotelian dictum of man as a social being applies also to the *homo religiosus*. The history and psychology of religion will attest to the fact that the force and effectiveness of religion grows commensurately with increasing participation of the entire society in the religious drama, with continuing embodiment of its formless subjectivity and with the expansion of objectified form and symbol.[93]

*Second, as we have already indicated, all attempts to divorce subjectivity from objective standards and postulates have been fraught with menace to ethical and cultural advancement.* This is singularly true in the case of religion. When intercourse with God is divorced from its social and communal aspects and concrete normative action, religion may develop into a barbaric, deleterious force. The unguided, inward life leads to the renunciation of ethical authority and moral awareness. Authority and unconditioned obedience form the background of the religious act. The elimination of the "ought" in religion is synonymous with its corruption.

*Third, the character of religion is exoteric.* The religious act must be accessible to every member of the human race, philosopher and tyro alike. Aristocracy in the religious realm is identical with the decadence of religion. Whatever the *telos* of religion, be it salvation, perfection, or ontological redemption, it is the dispensation of all mankind. The introduction of spiritualistic interpretations into religion renders the religious act esoteric. Religious introspection is not universal but depends largely upon the uniqueness of individual mentalities. Reflection and self-communion are not among the salient features of modern man. If the modern *homo sapiens* is to participate fully in the religious performance, then objective forms and principles must supplement subjectivity. The exoteric objective series is far more universal than recondite subjectivity.

The existence of an objective order in the religious sphere is a *conditio sine qua non* if religion is to play any role in the progress of human society. In this respect, religious liberalism has erred. It has underestimated the role of the norm and its correlation with the corporeal realm. Even when liberalism was inclined to tolerate the religious norm, it sought to relegate it to the sphere of the ethos. The uniqueness of the religious "ought", revealed in ritual and cult, was ignored.

In recapitulation we are confronted with a duality in the religious realm similar to that existing in science and other fields of human cultural endeavor. Reconstruction, a dominant methodological principle in philosophy, must be applied in the religious domain. There is no direct approach to pure religious subjectivity. Objective forms must be postulated as a point of departure, and by moving in the minus direction, one may gradually reconstruct underlying subjective aspects. Objectivity explored in retrospect yields subjectivity; other methods are fruitless.

The objective religious order is identical with the psychophysical religious act in which the living historical religious consciousness comes to expression. Just as the most concrete expression of art is to be found in books, paintings, etc., so is the most reliable sources of religious objective constructs to be discovered in religious literature containing norms, dogmas, postulates, etc. The canonized Scriptures serve as the most reliable standard of reference for objectivity. Through the method of reconstruction, God's word, the "letter of the scriptures, becomes an inner word, a certainty, insight, confession" of the God-thirsty soul. *Deus dixit* is the only objective source of all apocalyptic religion.

### PART FOUR

# THE HALAKHIC MIND

# I

OBJECTIFICATION reaches its highest expression in the Halakhah. Halakhah is the act of seizing the subjective flow and converting it into enduring and tangible magnitudes. It is the crystallization of the fleeting individual experience into fixed principles and universal norms. In short, Halakhah is the objectifying instrument of our religious consciousness, the form-principle of the transcendental act, the matrix in which the amorphous religious hylo is cast.

Rabbinic legalism, so derided by theologians, is nothing but an exact method of objectification, the modes of our response to what supremely impresses us. It is interesting to note that the Halakhah frequently operates with quantitative standards. It attempts not only to objectify religiosity, but also to quantify it. The act of measurement is a cardinal principle in Halakhah, and the religious experience is often quantified and mathematically determined. Reminiscent of Galileo's dictum, the "book" of Halakhah is replete with "triangles, circles and squares." Hence the reconstruction of subjective aspects within the objective halakhic order is far more complicated than that of the ordinary religious act. There is enormous distance between halakhic objectivity and its subjective counterpart.

Retrospective analysis opens new vistas to the philosopher of religion. The modern philosophy of religion is neither apologetic, agnostic nor mystic. It has a cognitive claim and a methodology of its own. It is not interested in the genetic approach to the religious act, nor does it raise the old problem of causality. It by-passes the "how" question and turns it over to explanatory psychology.[94] The focal problem is of a descriptive nature: What is the religious act? What is its structure, context and meaning?

As we have pointed out in the aforegoing chapters, the scientist operates with two subjective "orders," the antecedent, sensuous variety $A_1$ and the reconstructed structural aspect $A_2$. The objective additive order A lies between these two orders. Yet, the scientist conceives the relation between subjective $A_1$ and objective A differently from the A and $A_2$. While there is no causal link between summative A and its "antecedent" $A_1$, there is a definite causal relation between objective A and reconstructed $A_2$. This relation found its expression in the Eigenfunctions of quantum mechanics where the whole $A_2$ determines the particles of A. The philosopher of religion in adopting the scientific method of reconstruction, should equate the parallelism of the subjective and objective orders with the relation existing between primordial $A_1$ and postulated A which is non-causalistic. The method of modern physics should be emulated only partially, namely, the principle of reconstruction should be adopted while the causal survey should be rejected. In this respect the metaphysical thesis that the problem of philosophy is not the "how" but the "what" is correct.

The philosopher of religion in his regressive movement from objectivity to subjectivity should not undertake the explanation of religious norms by antecedence, for there is no causal continuity in the passage from one order to another. The subjective correlate does not interpret an objective commandment. The reconstruction method is recommended, but it cannot generate a causal explanation of religion.

At this point many philosophers have blundered. The curse of the "why" question followed them relentlessly. As soon as they had begun to interpret religious phenomena causally, they negated their very object. The chief error of genetics can be clarified by reference to Hume's psychological genetics. Hume disparaged human knowledge because he detected psychological roots at the base of all elementary structural concepts. The old myth of medieval scholasticism still held the upper hand in Hume's positivism. Whatever is true must be innate or given a priori; whatever was developed is false. Innate ideas present the design of genuineness and adequacy. Hence, as soon as Hume discovered the psychological origin of our cognitive propositions, his faith in their validity and objectivity was shattered. The categories were declared subjective and arbitrary—mere beliefs. Advocates of psychologism and positivism still travel the same road. The truth of the matter is that the genetic background of a certain method does not in the least affect its cogency and validity. The logical norm was never considered a function of psychological antecedent factors. Of course, the psychical act circumscribes the logical judgment which is an integral part of the former, but this does not exclude logical validity and cognitive worth.[95] In this sense, the Kantian a priori differs from the medieval innate ideas. Scholasticism spoke of ideas which were implanted in the human psyche and were not determined by anthropological emergence. Kantian a priorism in conjunction with its transcendental method does not pretend to ignore the genesis of knowledge and to claim miraculous origin for its basic methods. It merely divorces the psychological genetic viewpoint from the logical normative aspect. The "logos" as a normative agent is still authoritative regardless of its "biography." Whatever be the psychological history of geometry, Pythagoras' theorem is autonomously valid. The criterion of evidence and adequacy is not the transcendent source, but the indispensability of certain concepts and their constitutive experience. The task of the logician and the philosopher is not to survey the cognitive act from a causal, but from a normative and descriptive perspective. The genetic problem is the concern of the anthropologist and explanatory psychologist but not of the philosopher. Now it follows that, if sociological and psychological genetics are irrelevant to the philosophy of science, there is no reason for the philosopher of religion to limit his interpretation to causal designs. Unfortunately, while neither the mathematician nor physicist are troubled by the history of their disciplines, the philosopher of religion is still a slave to genetics.[96] In contrast with genetic methodology, a philosophy of religion, following a retrospective procedure —from the objective to the subjective realm—does not eliminate its own object. The method of reconstruction yields more than relational explanatory exposition. It offers a multidimensional religious outlook to the *homo religiosus*.

## II

THE basic error of religious liberalism is to be discerned less in its ideology than in its methodical approach. Liberalism has travelled in the wrong direction—from subjectivity to objectivity—and in so doing his misconstrued both. Religious liberalism is based upon a very "simple" methodological principle. Subjective religiosity, the moderns, say, is subordinated to the omnipotent authority of time and change. It is impossible therefore to consider any set of religious norms and dogmas as immutable, for the objective order moving parallel to the subjective undergoes the same metamorphoses. Let us admit that modern religious subjectivism is indeed incommensurable with the objective order sanctioned by tradition. One is still tempted to ask how the fathers of contemporary liberalism intend to mould a modern religious act out of the "new" chaotic mass of subjectivity? The method of objectification is, of course, at their disposal. They may project subjective flux upon externality and create a new, artificial objective order. But this very method is fallacious. If, for example, a certain school of liberal thought asserts that the traditional dogmas pertaining to the essence and attributes of God are not acceptable to the scientific mind, then the question arises: What type of divinity is to be offered as a substitute for the traditional God? In other words, what method of construction is to be applied in forming a modern theology? We know that such a school will always begin with the subjective domain. It will perhaps claim to have analyzed the deepest strata of the religious consciousness and to have examined the God-thirsty soul with all its conflicting emotions and paradoxical sentiments. Out of such hyletic matter liberalism attempts to mould a new deity which is half pantheistic and half moralistic. The ultra modern God is both a metaphysical *élan vital* and a cosmic moral *telos*.[97]

The fallacy of this movement lies in its utter lack of methodology. Where is the assurance that these philosophers, while exploring modern religious subjectivism, have not erred and strayed? Columbus of old, sailing an

uncharted sea, mistook the American continent for the
"Indies." The liberals of today, instead of religious subjectivity, plunge mistakenly into some other subjective "order"
—the moral or aesthetic. There being no boundary lines in
the subjective sphere, trespasses upon the territory of ethics
and aesthetics occur unwittingly. When viewed from any
other aspect but the objective, subjectivity does not present
separate realism. It is only the act of a retrospective analysis
that classifies religiosity. Religious subjectivity is synonymous with the subjective "order" surveyed from the premises of objectivity. If one seeks primordial subjectivity he
would find an evanescent flux, neither religious nor mundane, but, similar to Aristotelian matter, unregulated and
chaotic. If an objective compass be lacking, the final port
of landing is uncertain.[98]

Liberalism has approached its subject matter with bias. It
has boldy declared traditional dogmas to be incongruous
with modern subjectivism. Actually, they have neither
examined that ancient order of subjectivity out of which
these "old-fashioned" concepts of God have evolved, nor
have they investigated the religiosity of modern man. This
being the case, the abandonment of certain traditional
concepts in favor of more modern ones is nothing but
sheer whimsicality if not foolhardy iconoclasm.

If the commensurability of traditional beliefs with modern religious experience is to be investigated, the method
of retrospective exploration—the regressive movement
from objective religious symbols to subjective flux—must
be applied.

For were we to analyze the mystery of the God-man relation as reflected in the Jewish religious consciousness from
both traditional and modern aspects, it would be necessary
that we first gather all objectified data at our disposal:

passages in the Holy Writ pertaining to divinity and divine attributes; the norms regulating the God-man contact such as the norm of love and fear of God; moments of tension between God and man, as in the case of Job; many halakhic problems where certain attitudes of man towards Divinity have found their expression; all forms of cult, liturgy, prayer, Jewish mysticism, rational philosophy, religious movements, etc. Out of this enormous mass of objectified constructs, the underlying subjective aspects could gradually be reconstructed. The latter, in turn, should be compared to central structural facts of modern psychology, typology and the philosophy of religion. It is not too far fetched to anticipate the result of such an inquiry and predict that the traditional intimate God-man communion would not be as simple and naive as the moderns would have us imagine. It is very doubtful whether the highly developed modern mind would reject such a concept of a personal God in intercourse with man as one that would "mislead the simple and alienate the sophisticated." The scope of this essay does not permit of a detailed analysis of the concept of God in the Jewish religion. However, the methodological error at the root of reform ideology is clear.

## III

ALTHOUGH the method of reconstruction can be adopted and utilized by any theistic religion, it is of immense importance in the field of Jewish philosophy. One of the most perplexing problems that has confused the

finest of minds is that of the rationalization of the commandments (טעמי המצוות). The difficulties encountered by
Maimonides in his attempt to eliminate Saadiah and Bahya's
dualism[99] of Rational and Traditional commandments
(שמעיות and שכליות), and to develop an all-embracing interpretation of religious norms are well known. Twenty-five
chapters of the *Guide* are devoted exclusively to the solution
of this problem. However, Maimonides' attempt at rationalization, more so than any other of his theoretical undertak-
ings, brought forth a historical controversy that embroiled
all Jewish scholars of that epoch, dividing them into two
factions: The Maimunists and Anti-Maimunists. Judging
Maimonides' undertaking retrospectively, one must admit
that the master whose thought shaped Jewish ideology for
centuries to come did not succeed in making his interpretation of the commandments prevalent in our world perspective. While we recognize his opinions on more complicated problems such as prophecy, teleology and creation,
we completely ignore most of his rational notions regarding
the commandments. The reluctance on the part of the
Jewish *homo religiosus* to accept Maimonidean rationalistic
ideas is not ascribable to any agnostic tendencies, but to
the incontrovertible fact that such explanations neither
edify nor inspire the religious consciousness. They are
essentially, if not entirely, valueless for the religious
interests we have most at heart. Maimonides' failure to
impress his rationalistic method upon the vivid religious
consciousness is to be attributed mainly to the fact that the
central theme of the Maimonidean exposition is the causalistic problem. The "how" question, the explanatory quest,
and the genetic attitude determined Maimonides' doctrine
of the commandments. Instead of describing, Maimonides
explained; instead of reconstructing, he constructed.[100]

As we have previously indicated, whenever the causal question is raised, the philosopher must transcend the boundary line of religion in order to find his answer which lies beyond the religious domain. Both mechanistic and teleological concepts of causality explain the effect through the existence of an alien factor, be it within or without the system. Thus religion cannot be interpreted under immanent aspects but must avail itself of foreign elements. The net result of Maimonides' rationalization is that religion no longer operates with unique autonomous norms, but with technical rules, the employment of which would culminate in the attainment of some extraneous maximum bonum. In rationalizing the commandments genetically, Maimonides developed a religious "instrumentalism."[101] Causality reverted to teleology (the Aristotelian concept of *causa finalis*) and Jewish religion was converted into technical wisdom.

For example, should we post the question: why did God forbid perjury? the intellectualistic philosopher would promptly reply, "because it is contrary to the norm of truth." Thus, he would explain a religious norm by an ethical precept, making religion the handmaid of ethics. Again, when the same philosopher attempts to sanction dietary laws on hygienic grounds, the specific religious content and meaning are supplanted by a principle of foreign extraction. If the Sabbath is to be seen only against the background of mundane social justice and similar ideals, the intrinsic quality of the Sabbath is transformed into something alien. It serves merely as a means to the realization of a "higher" end. Maimonides' efforts foreshadowed failure from the very outset of his "how" approach.

It is worthy of note that Maimonides, the halakhic scholar, came nearer the core of philosophical truth than

Maimonides, the speculative philosopher. In contradistinction to the causal method of the philosophical *Guide* that leads to a religious *techné*, the halakhic *Code* (the *Mishneh Torah*) apprehends the religious act in an entirely different light. The *Code* does not pursue the objective causation of the commandment, but attempts to reconstruct its subjective correlative. It would seem that the Maimonides of the Halakhah was not intrigued by the "how" question. He freed himself from the genetic purview and employed a descriptive method of expounding the content and symbolic meaning of the religious norm. The "what'"question was his guide in the *Code*.

To illustrate the methodological difference between the *Guide* and the *Code,* we may cite three examples. First, the norm of the Shofar as presented in the *Code*:

"Although the blowing of the shofar on Rosh Hashanah is a decree of the Holy Writ, nevertheless there is a hint to it, as if saying, 'Ye that sleep, bestir yourselves from your sleep, and ye that slumber, emerge from your slumber. Examine your conduct, return in repentance and remember your Creator'" (*Teshuvah* III,4).[102]

Let us carefully examine Maimonides' words. When he begins with the reservation that the sounding of the shofar on Rosh Hashanah is a decree of the Holy Writ, he means to eliminate the "how" question. We are not to ask for any generating cause or goals. This is implied in the halakhic dictum, "I have set down statutes and you may not examine them." (חקים חקקתי ואין לך רשות להרהר אחריהם). But the verb "examine," הרהר, with the addition of the prepositional phrase (in the Hebrew) אחריהם (literally: "after them"), denotes causal criticism—the examination of the motives and causes of the norm. Thus Maimonides, at the very beginning of the paragraph, excludes any question of causal interpretation. The concept of גזירת הכתוב (decree of the Writ) renders such an approach impossible. However, by continuing רמז יש בו, "there is a hint (*in* this command-ment)," he leads us into a new realm of philosophical her-meneutics. Causality and teleology of the norm lie beyond us. However, the hints and allusions hidden in them are open to our view. What is the difference between a "cause" and a "hint"? The distinction between them is the same as that between the methods of objectification and recon-struction. By establishing the cause, one objectifies the datum and subordinates it to a superior order. However, by exploring the norm retrospectively through vectorial hints which point toward subjectivity, the religious act with its unique structure retains its full autonomy. Had Maimonides adopted Saadiah's reasons[103] for the sounding of the shofar and held that it is reminiscent of an ancient nomadic period when it served either as a signal for alarm or as a summons to joyous celebration, he would have been entrapped in the same causal maze as that of his *Guide*. Yet, here he ignores the historical motive and interprets the shofar purely from a symbolic aspect. His view that the shofar *alludes* to repentance and self-examination is not a classical causal interpretation based upon a two-val-ued logic which entails necessity. The mechanistic relation between A and B is unique and necessary. However, there is no relational necessity between the sounding of the shofar and conversion. It does not follow that the sounding of the shofar is a necessary and sufficient means for the end of inspiring man to penitence and conversion. The call to repent could have been realized in many ways and there is no necessary reason why the Torah selected the means of the sounding of the shofar. Hence the message of repentence, which for Maimonides is implied in the sounding of the shofar, cannot serve as the cause of the commandment that would assure it a status of necessity, but it must be apprehended rather as an allusion to a correlated subjective aspect. *Kol shofar*, the sound of the shofar, only betokens self-examination and conversion. The reconstruction method does not operate with the principle of necessity. It neither claims that the subjective counterpart would only be crystallized in one particular way, nor does it explain how it was finally reflected in its objectified form. It merely points at the stationary trail left behind the religious "logos" and indicates parallel tendencies in both the subjective and objective orders.

A second illustration from Maimonides' *Code* is the norm of catharsis:

"It is apparent that contamination and purification constitute a decree of the Holy Writ, and they are not among the things which human reason can understand; they are among the non-rational laws (חוקים). Purification by immersion belongs to this class of laws, for contamination is neither of dirt nor of offal which can be washed away with water. Nevertheless a hint is contained in this. . . ." (*Mikvaoth* XI, 12).[104]

Again we encounter the same approach. The causal method is rejected, for catharsis is not a rational norm within the grasp of finite reason. The method of reconstruction is again employed to analyze the norm and discover the hint leading to the subjective realm. In the case of catharsis, according to Maimonides, the arrow points towards the symbolic role ascribed to water by the Jewish religious consciousness. We could for instance, as many have done, interpret the laws of contamination and purification from a causal, technical viewpoint. We could introduce either hygienic and sanitary considerations or those of primitive tabooism and make the idea of catharsis plausible to the average man. But the profound religious mind would undoubtedly resent such platitudes. The *homo religiosus* would be averse to an approach which does not circumscribe the religious act, but deprives it of its meaningful content and ignores its essential significance.

A third illustration is that of the Sabbath norm. Maimonides' treatment in the *Guide* of the Sabbath precept instances another contrast between these methods:

"The idea of Sabbath, its interpretation, is clear to everyone and does not require elucidation. We know that Sabbath means rest; hence one seventh of man's life is spent in comfort,[105] in rest, free from the worries and cares to which both great and small are subject. The Sabbath also perpetuates and forever confirms the very sublime idea, namely, faith in the divine act of creation" (*Guide* III, 43).[106]

Maimonides here offers two possible aspects from which the Sabbath may be viewed. One is based upon divine benevolence which, in this instance, allots man a full measure of happiness for one seventh of his life span. The other, which is borrowed from the Scriptures and which Maimonides adopted in the *Code*,[107] is of symbolic strain: the Sabbath symbolizes the act of creation. The first, yields a purely pragmatic interpretation; the goal of the Sabbath is hedonic, and the means leading to its realization belong to a religious technical discipline. Thus the Sabbath idea is dispossessed of its breadth and warmth. The metaphysical sweep is checked and the religious ardor is cooled. Yet, the second interpretation, envisaging the Sabbath as the incarnation of the mystery of creation, penetrates infinity itself. It discovers in dead matter and mechanical motion the fingerprints of a Creator and the contours of a conscious creation. The covenant-idea and the incomprehensible God-man contact emerge in full refulgence. It is superfluous to state that the *homo religiosus* finds delight in such an interpretation, however "naive," rather than in a pragmatic and technical scheme devised with so much prudence and calculation.

There are innumerable illustrations of these two varied methods of approach to the religious act.[108] It has already been made clear that philosophically the causalistic method invariably leads to circumrotary explanation, and never to penetrative description. The enumeration of causes never exhausts the eidetic substance itself. It discloses the "what has gone before" but never the "is" of the subject matter.[109] The only method open is the retrospective which explores the objective series for the sake of excavating hidden strata underlying these objective forms.

The solution to the old philosophical problem regarding the rationalization of religion can be formulated, then, in the following manner. If rationalizaton is guided by the "how" question and by the principle of objectification, then it is detrimental to religious thought. If, however, the lodestar of rationalization is the "what" question, and its method is identical with descriptive reconstruction, then it may enrich our knowledge of the *homo religiosus*. Hence a system of commandment rationalization (טעמי המצוות) is a philosophical possibility if it is determined by descriptive hermeneutics. Of course, we cannot expect to bring the descriptive method to full perfection in the domain of religion by reason of the paradoxical character of the religious experience. We shall always be confronted with incongruities and inconsistencies. Science was, has been, and will be more successful in this respect for its method is relational (not eidetic) construction and reconstruction. However, by continuous observation and analysis of the objectified forms of the religious act, the general tendencies and trends latent in the religious consciousness may be grasped.

Despite its shortcomings, the retrospective procedure still remains the only method to be pursued by the *homo religio-*
*sus* if he is indeed bent on describing the religious act. If the philosophy of religion asks for example, how the *homo religiosus* interprets the concepts of time, space, causality, substance, ego, etc.,[110] then it would have to look into the objective series and examine norms, beliefs, articles of faith, religious texts, etc. Out of this objectified material, the philosopher of religion may glean some hints regarding the structure of the most basic religious cognitive concepts. The objective act alone may serve as a point of departure for the philosopher desirous of interpreting the religious experience.

In particular does this hold true of the Jewish religion where the process of objectification culminates in the Halakhah. We do not know of any other religion where the process of objectification has attained such completeness as it does in the Halakhah.

## IV

IT is pertinent to note that most modern Jewish philosophers have adopted a very unique method. The source
of knowledge, for them, is Medieval Jewish philosophy.
The living historical religious consciousness which
embraces both antiquity and modern times is ignored.
Such a method cannot cope with the problems of Jewish
philosophy for three reasons. First, medieval Jewish
thought, despite its accomplishment and merit, has not
taken deep root in Jewish historical religious realism and
has not shaped Jewish religious world perspective. When
we speak of philosophy of religion, we must have in mind
foremost the philosophy of religious realities experienced
by the entire community, and not some abstract metaphysics cultived by an esoteric group of philosophers. Second, we know that the most central concepts of medieval
Jewish philosophy are rooted in ancient Greek and
medieval Arabic thought and are not of Jewish origin at
all. It is impossible to reconstruct a unique Jewish world
perspective out of alien material. Third, the Hegelian thesis
that philosophy is synonymous with *fieri*, continuous process and activity, was borne out by contemporary scientific
facts and has become a truism in modern philosophy. If
Jewish philosophy is reduced to obsolete concepts and
medieval categories that time has rendered sterile, then
where is living philosophical continuity? Even were we to
demonstrate greater magnanimity and introduce modern

Jewish philosophical advancements as a point of departure for the reconstruction of a Jewish world perspective, we would not meet the requirements of historical continuity. Since the time of the great medieval philosophers, Jewish philosophical thought has expressed itself only sporadically and then in a fragmentary manner, and this largely upon premises which were more non-Jewish than Jewish. The most characteristic example is to be found in Hermann Cohen's *philosophy of religion*, which, for him, was identical with *the* philosophy of the Jewish religion. There are many truths in his interpretation, but the main trends are idealistic Kantian and not Jewish.

When we apply typological standards to a philosophy, two important factors must be borne in mind: First, the central problem typifies the form-whole. It lends uniqueness to the philosophical thought. The question charts the course of the philosopher. Descartes was intrigued by the problem of cogency and reality, Spinoza by that of substance and infinity, Kant by that of a priori knowledge, Hume by that of experience, etc. Second, the structural patterns of the system: Single thoughts do not determine the singularity of a philosophy. The organic whole, with its morphological designs and Gestalt qualities, is decisive.

To this end there is only a single source from which a Jewish philosophical *Weltanschauung* could emerge; the objective order—the Halakhah. In passing onward from the Halakhah and other objective constructs to a limitless subjective flux, we might possibly penetrate the basic structure of our religious consciousness. We might also evolve cognitive tendencies and aspects of our world interpretation and gradually grasp the mysteries of the religious halakhic act. Problems of freedom, causality, God-man relationship, creation, and nihility would be illuminated by halakhic principles. A new light could be shed on our apprehension of reality. The halakhic compass would also guide us through the lanes of medieval philosophy and reveal structural standards by which to judge and evaluate the philosophical thought of that golden age. It would help us discriminate between the living and the dead in Jewish philosophy. What, for instance, is of halakhic nature in the *Guide* and the *Kuzari*, and what merely an echo of Platonic-Aristotelian philosophy? The purpose of such an analysis is not to eliminate non-Jewish elements. Far from it, for the blend of Greek and Jewish thought has oftimes been truly magnificent. However, by tracing the Jewish trends and comparing them to the non-Jewish, we shall enrich our outlook and knowledge. Modern Jewish philosophy must be nurtured on the historical religious consciousness that has been projected onto a fixed objective screen.

Out of the sources of Halakhah, a new world view awaits formulation.

*Notes*

# PART I

1. The term *homo religiosus* is used throughout to denote the religious personality. In the comparative science of religion, the term usually signifies the founder of a religion.

2. V. Ferdinand Lassalle, *Herakleitos der Dunkle*. His view, however, was not adopted by the historians of philosophy.

3. This is perhaps the reason for Aristotelian philosophy becoming the clearing house for Greek thought. Aristotle, as a professed empiricist, succeeded in formulating a scientific world-explanation which embraced the universe in its totality. Before Aristotle, Greek scientific thought was essentially rhapsodic. It lacked the aspect of totality and, therefore, could not attain the heights which it did in the Peripatetic school where science was the canvas upon which Aristotle painted his philosophic panorama. Lacking a scientific exposition of reality, ancient Greek philosophy, in its attempt at understanding and grasping the ontological mystery, moved in a vacuum.

4. One observes in *The Critique of Pure Reason* that much as Kant differed from Newton on the problem of the absolute character of time and space, he nevertheless interpreted them in terms of the mathematician and physicist. He saw in the intuition of space the order and peculiarities of the Euclidean space, and in the time-awareness a one-dimensional succession identical for him with the succession of mathematical points on a line. The categories of "Pure Reason," like causality, substance, necessity, etc., were similarly molded by Kant to fit into the framework constructed by the physicist. Kant considered it his philosophical mission to find an adequate metaphysical frame for Newton's *Principia*. This endeavour of giving legitimate philosophical expression to the mathematical sciences

became the central axis of the Neo-Kantian school. Hermann Cohen, with fanatical devotion to the supremacy of the mathematico-scientific process of cognition, considered the latter the ultimate ground of reality; he ascribed almost "divine" attributes to scientific reason.

5. The Aristotelian view was much closer to the natural world than that of Plato, for whom sensible phenomena and abstract ideas belonged to two different orders.

6. An exception to this rule is to be found in the philosophy of Berkeley. Berkeley absolutized the sensuous qualities by transferring them to an infinite, divine consciousness. This blend of sensualism and idealism has no counterpart in other idealistic schools.

7. When we speak of philosophic idealism, we must not confuse the concept of idealism in epistemology with that in metaphysics. Epistemological idealism denotes the coordination of reality with thinking, while metaphysical idealism conceives the spirit as the essence of reality.

8. A noteworthy exception among metaphysical spiritualists is the Hegelian school which did not adopt the scientific approach to reality.

9. *Bulletin de la Societe Francaise de Philosophie*, June 1901; A.D. Lindsay, *The Philosophy of Bergson*, p. 11.

10. As a matter of fact, British Neo-Kantians and Neo-Hegelians such as Andrew Seth Pringle-Pattison, the brothers R. B. and J. S. Haldane, *et al.*, discovered, as early as the eighties of the last century, the inadequacy of the Newtonian-Kantian mechanical categories for the interpretation of the phenomena of life and mind. English non-scientific metaphysics of the Absolute (inspired by Lotze) is much older than its Continental counterpart. Bradley's ethical studies which appeared in the seventies sponsored a new metaphysical epoch. What is more, it had already dawned on Carlyle in 1829 that from the time of Locke, metaphysics traveled along a physical and mechanical route, ignoring the mind. Nevertheless, no one formulated the discrepancy between the method of the mathematician and that of the biologist and psychologist as ably, clearly and unequivocally as did Bergson. His blend of pragmatism and absolutism in particular stimulated philosophical thought. Cf. John H. Muirhead, *The Platonic Tradition in Anglo-Saxon Philosophy*, pp. 130; 174-181.

11. The most conspicuous illustration of the incommensurability of philosophy with modern physical magnitudes is Whitehead's abortive attempt to eliminate bifurcation of nature and to create a monistic reality. In order to bridge the gap separating the experiences of the

apparent world from the postulated reality introduced by classical and modern physics, he attempted to derive the scientific constructs from our individual experience, and to evolve the mathematical physical space and time out of the intuited and "distorted" space-time awareness by which we coordinate our daily life. This endeavor led his theory into conflict with the Einsteinian theory of relativity in its most pivotal points such as the concept of simultaneity which Einstein interprets in terms of light propagation (special theory of relativity) and the heterogeneity of the space-time continuum (general theory of relativity). This controversy resulted in Whitehead's dismissal of the formula of relativity and the principle of simultaneity on the grounds that the modern epistemologist may follow his own method. It should be borne in mind that Whitehead came to philosophy from mathematics and physics. Vide A. Einstein and others, *The Principle of Relativity* (London; 1923), p. 183. Compare with A. Whitehead, *The Principle of Relativity*. Also see A. Eddington, *The Nature of the Physical World*, pp. 145-146; B. Russell, *Analysis of Matter*, p. 78; Filmer S. E. Northrop. "Whitehead's Philosophy of Science," in *Library of Living Philosophers*, vol. III.

12. The sensible world which Berkeley absolutized found its modern expounders in phenomenologists like Husserl, Scheler, Hartmann, and others. The "saving of the appearances" became the prime task of contemporary Neo-Hegelians and neo-realists. Whitehead's attempt to rehabilitate the "distorted private" universe is well known. However, neo-realists measured sense-data with a semi-physical yardstick. Cf. R.F. Hoernle, *Studies in Contemporary Metaphysics*, V.

13. *Ibid*, chap. II, "The Idol of Scientific Method".

14. Some of the modern positivists do not eliminate (as Hume did) the concept of the real, although they consider the metaphysical problem as pseudo-scientific. See, for example, R. Carnap, *Der Logische Aufbau der Welt*, pp. 237-272; M. Schlick, *Allgemeine Erkenntnislehre*, p. 172 *et seq.*

15. In surveying cognitive pluralism against its historic background, one becomes aware of the fact that this problem is a legacy from ancient and medieval thought. Plato's four-fold classification of knowledge; Aristotle's various divisions of cognition; Saadiah and Maimonides' different cognitive sources; Descartes' deduction and intuition; Spinoza's cognitive triad of *opinio, ratio* and *intuitio*; Schelling's artistic intuition, etc. — these form the historical canvas upon which modern pluralism has been so strikingly projected. Yet, there is

a basic difference between the philosophical tradition concerning multifarious knowledge and contemporary non-scientific metaphysics. Classical epistemology, though discriminating between many cognitive methods, did not conceive knowledge as a manifold. It rather apprehended the latter as a hierarchy, in the sense that there are lower and higher degrees of cognition. In the final analysis, all aspects culminate in one apex. Modern pluralism, however, does not recognize any superiority of degree in the cognitive field. There is neither cognitive ascent or descent. Our multi-methodological approach is warranted by a proliferation of aspects inherent in reality itself; or by a multitude of interests latent in the cognitive act, be it of a purely contingent pragmatic or absolute order. Among classical philosophers, Blaise Pascal approaches our modern viewpoint most strikingly. Of course, there are certain sections of Pascal's *Pensees* that remind us of Descartes' deduction and intuition, and of Aristotle's primary principles or immediate premises. Yet some passages reflect in unequivocal manner an attitude akin to modern pluralism. There is little wonder that Max Scheler considers Pascal the father of emotional apriorism. To illustrate the dualism in Pascal's philosophy, two excerpts are here quoted.

"We know truth not only through the reason but also through the heart; it is from the latter source that we know its first principles and it is useless for reasoning that has no share in them to attempt to oppose them...Knowledge of the first principles like that of space, time, motion, number, is as positive as that of any given us by our reasoning and it is upon the knowledge of the heart and instinct that reason must rest and found all its conclusions...The heart feels that there are three dimensions in space and that numbers are infinite; reason afterwards demonstrates...Principles are felt—propositions concluded."

Nothing new or exciting is revealed in this passage. The fact that first postulates are somehow immediately apprehended was already known to ancient philosophers. Pascal only substitutes the heart for immediate knowledge not subject to demonstration. We may conceive Pascal's feeling and reasons of the heart as metaphors only. Another passage, however, throws a different light upon this mathematician-philosopher.

"The will is one of the principle instruments of belief...things are true or false according to the aspect in which we regard them. The will which is more inclined to one thing than another, turns away the mind from the consideration of those things which it likes not to contemplate, and thus the mind, moving with the will, stops to observe that which it approves and forms its judgments by what it sees."

Modern perspectivism, which sees in the act of cognition a concomitant of a valuing act that occurs under certain practical and teleological aspects, comes to the fore in Pascal's last quoted words. These sound like Bergsonian prose. In sum, approval or disapproval precede any cognitive act. The reason is the instrument of the will, and the theoretical act is subordinated to the volitional. The question that arises is, on what premise does the will base its approval or reproach? Pascal in all likelihood turns for help to the "heart" and its "reasons." The latter appear to be cognitive volitional patterns according to which the will molds its acceptance or disapproval. In such a context, "reason of the heart" is not a mere metaphor denoting rational immediate knowledge (of Aristotelian and Cartesian strain), for this type of cognition follows upon the volitional decision and is not antecedent to the will; but rather represents specific cognitive designs that govern man's volitional and emotional life. Cf., Blaise Pascal, *The Thoughts, Letters and Opuscules* (New York: 1861), p. 516; *Pensees*, Modern Library Edition, p. 3.

16. Santayana discriminated between legitimate metaphysics, consisting in the acceptance of science "while its present results are modified by suggesting speculatively what its ultimate results might be," and illegitimate metaphysics that departs from scientific standards. Yet Santayana's philosophic career refutes his faith in scientific metaphysics. Whereas, during the reign of *Reason in Science*, he firmly believed that there is no knowledge different methodologically from the scientific, he later did an about-face in *Skepticism and Animal Faith* and brought forth, in a defiant mood, the heresy that the scientific method is not universal. In this quasi-skeptical period, he maintained that the concepts of science are mere symbols that provide us with useful knowledge. "The pride of science should turn into humility ...the forms of science are optional...Science yields practical assurances couched in symbolic terms, but no ultimate insight." See Santayana, *Reason in Science*, pp. 18-36, 301; *Some Turns of Thought in Modern Philosophy*. p. 79. See also Charles Hartshorne, *Animal Faith and the Art of Intuition*; Sterling P. Lamprecht, *Santayana's Doctrine of Essence*; Milton K. Munitz, "Ideals and Essences in Santayana's Philosophy," in *Library of Living Philosophers*, vol. II.

Santayana's eternal essences are apprehended by the mind in our intuitive experience. Such a non-scientific experience could be adopted by Scheler and Hartmann without reservation.

17. Likewise, we find a pluralistic attitude in F.C.S. Schiller's Humanist Voluntarism. Moreover, he would tolerate a metaphysics of ultimate reality. See "Why Humanism?" in *Contemporary British Philosophy* (first series), pp. 387-409.

18. John Dewey, although a militant crusader of pragmatism, did not align himself with pluralistic ideologies. His faith in scientific progress which adjusts itself to ever-changing "situations" remained unshaken.

19. Of course, many philosophers, like Russell, Santayana (in his first stage) and others who combine positivism with its anti-thesis, neo-realism, will vehemently protest any heretic leanings of the philosopher. Yet, positivism, surveyed critically, leads to Hume's skepticism rather than to scientific neo-realism. James' keen analysis of a pluralistic pragmatism is by far superior to a monistic physicalism.

20. Cassirer discriminates between the scientific "logos" which knows that it operates with symbols, and other cognitive agents which are not aware of that. Yet scientific copy realism does not bear out this thesis. It has never been conscious of the symbolic character of physical knowledge.

21. Johannes von Uexküell, as a champion of vitalism, developed a biological scheme of a heterogeneous reality. V. Johannes von Uexküell, *Theoretische Biologie (Berlin: 1938); Unwelt und Innerwelt der Tiere*, (1909).

22. Nuclear physics has given tremendous impetus to this trend.

23. Compare Russell's statement, "geometry throws no more light on the nature of space than arithmetic throws upon the population of the United States." *Mysticism and Logic* (1921), pp. 92-94. See Whitehead, *The Axioms of Projective Geometry* (Cambridge: 1906) and *The Axioms of Descriptive Geometry* (Cambridge: 1907).

24. Cf., E. Whittaker in *Philosophical Magazine and Journal of Science*, vols. III-IV, no. 231 (London: April 1943).

25. V. Eddington, *The Mathematical Theory of Relativity*, p. 2.

26. Cf. Louis de Broglie, *An Introduction to the Study of Wavemechanics*, p. 179.

27. "Das Quantenpostulat bedeutet, dass jede Beobachtung atomarer Phoenomene eine nicht zu vernachlaessigende Wechselwirkung mit dem Messungsmittel fordert, und dass also weder den

Phoenomenen noch dem Beobachtungsmittel eine selbstaendige physicalische Realitalet im gewoehnlichen Sinne zugeschrieben werden kann. Uleberhaupt enthaelt der Begriff der Beobachtung eine Willkuer, indem er wesentlich darauf beruht, welche Gegenstaende mit zu dem zu beobachtenden System gerchnet werden." N. Bohr. *Das Quantenpostulat und die Neuere Entwicklung der Atomistik Naturwissenschaften*, (1928). H. 15. See also his *Wirkungsquantum und Naturbeschreibung* (June 1929). Cf. Max Planck. *The Philosophy of Physics*, p. 102-103.

28. "Theoretical physics does not consider individual measurement as an event. ... By an event physics means a certain merely intellectual process. It substitutes a new world in place of that given to us by the senses or by the measuring instruments which are used in order to aid the senses. This other world is the so-called physical world-image; it is merely an intellectual structure. To a certain extent it is arbitrary. It is a kind of model or idealization created in order to avoid the inaccuracy inherent in every measurement and to facilitate exact definition. ... It is not therefore the case, as is sometimes stated, that the physical world image can or should contain only directly observable magnitudes. The contrary is the fact. The world image contains no observable magnitudes at all; all that it contains is symbols. More than this: it invariably contains certain components having no immediate meaning as applied to the world of the senses, nor indeed any meaning at all, e.g., either waves, partial oscillations, reference coordinates, etc. ... A superficial consideration shows how wide is the distance between the world image and the sense world of quantum physics and how much more difficult it is, in quantum physics, to translate an event from the world-image into the sense world and vice versa. Things are no longer as simple as they were in classical physics." Max Planck, *The Philosophy of Physics*, pp. 53-66. Compare the above statement with the attitude adopted by Heisenberg in *Matrix Mechanics*.

29. See Einstein's "Remarks on Bertrand Russell's Theory of Knowledge," and Russell's "Reply to Criticism," pp. 696-697, in *Library of Living Philosophers*, vol. V; also A. Einstein, *The World as I See It*. Einstein was careful to make the reservation that he speaks exclusively from a logical aspect. He did this so as not to confuse the logical thesis concerning the incommensurability of the scientific and sensible worlds with the standpoint of the psychologist who may perhaps find some genetic link between both. This is in complete harmony

with the Kantian a priori and transcendental method. Had Russell paid attention to this remark, he would not have raised his positivistic objections against Einstein's epistemological theory. In general, it is amusing to note how Einstein, the physicist, admits the symbolic nature of physical knowledge while Russell, the philosopher, attempts to derive it from sensory experience.

"Science is not just a collection of laws, a catalogue of unrelated facts. It is a creation of the human mind with its freely invented ideas and concepts. ... The background of all events was...the four dimensional space-time continuum, another free invention with new transformation properties. The quantum theory created new essential features of our reality. ... Without the belief that it is possible to grasp reality with our theoretical constructions...there could be no science. This belief is...the fundamental motive for all scientific creation." Einstein and Infeld, *The Evolution of Physics*, p. 310-313. Einstein's reliance on belief is reminiscent of Hume.

30. Analogous views were expounded by the leading physicists and mathematicians of the last century, such as Poincaré, Hertz, and Mach. V. Rousseau's Introduction to his *Discours sur L'origine et les Fondements de L'inégalité parmi les Hommes* where he describes the hypothetical method (*des raisannements hypothetique et conditionelles*) which was used by the fathers of classical physics.

31. "And yet in regard to the nature of things, this knowledge is only an empty shell—a form of symbols. ... All through the physical world runs that unknown content, which surely be the stuff of our consciousness. ... And, moreover, we have found that where science has progressed the farthest, the mind has but regained from nature that which that mind has put into nature. We have found a strange footprint on the shores of the unknown. We have devised profound theories, one after another, to account for its origin. At least we have succeeded in reconstructing the creature that made the footprints. And, lo! it is our own." Eddington, *Space, Time and Gravitation* (Cambridge: 1921), p. 200-201.

Kant's a priori could not come to the forefront of the scientific world more clearly and distinctly than in Eddington's last sentences. His dictum that we regain from nature what we put into it is a verbatim and literatim translation of Kant's famous answer to the question, "How are synthetic judgments a priori possible?" or "How are pure mathematics and physics possible?"

"Was Gegenstaende betrifft...so werden die Versuche, sie zu

denken. ... einen herrlichen Probierstein desjenigen abgeben, was wit als die veraenderte Methode der Denkungsart annehmen, dass wir naemlich von den Dingen nur das a priori erkennen was wir selbst in sie legen." *Critique of Pure Reason.* Preface to 2nd Edition.

32. Cf. J. Royce, *The Religious Aspect of Philosophy,* where the problem of religious postulation is discussed.

33. Modern psychology has contributed its share to the liberation of philosophy. As we have seen, recent developments in psychological analysis, Gestalt and child psychology have induced modern students to break with the atomistic, mosaic psychology of association. Many facts brought forth by observation did not fit into a monistic framework constructed by physiological psychology. The whole concept of perception and sense-experience has undergone a thorough revision that can hardly harmonize with naive naturalism and positivism. It appears that positivism has to face a two-front onslaught: from physical as well as psychological aspects.

34. Although Neo-Hegelian metaphysics (Bradley, Royce, Bosanquet, Hoernle, *et al.*) which identifies the real with the whole and the individual draws on all kinds of experience (logical, ethical and aesthetical), it is pledged nevertheless to a dualistic method: the sectional (scientific) and the synoptic (metaphysical). All great experiences converge into one total experience through which the universe reveals itself.

35. It is irrelevant whether the new methodology was formulated by the metaphysicians themselves under the aspect of the spirit (anglo-saxon Neo-Hegelianism, Bergsonian intuitionism, etc.) or borrowed directly from the humanist (Scheler, Hartmann, et al.) In both cases the unique exigencies of the spirit revealed to the philosopher the many-sided character of the cognitive affair.

36. Cf. Eduard Spranger, *Lebensformen,* Introduction.

37. "Laws of nature are merely generic notions for the changes in nature." Helmholtz, *Treatise on Physiological Optics* (1925), vol. III, pp. 33-35.

38. As to the space-time continuum of the special theory of relativity, all physicists agree that it displays absolute features. Einstein himself writes as follows: "Just as it was necessary from the Newtonian standpoint to make both the statements, *tempus est absolutum, spatium est absolutum,* so from the standpoint of the special theory of relativity we must say, *continuum spatii et temporis est absolutum.* In this latter statement *absolutum* means not only physically real but also independent of its physical properties, having a physical effect but not itself

influenced by physical conditions." *The Meaning of Relativity*, p. 61.

This definition cannot be applied to the space-time continuum of the general theory. For the latter not only acts upon matter, but is also affected by matter. And indeed the absolute character of such a space-time continuum is problematical. V. Einstein, Ibid, p. 62. In this regard, see Hermann Weyl, *Space-Time-Matter*, (who denies the absolute traits of the heterogeneous space-time continuum of the general theory); M. Planck, *Where Is Science Going?* (New York; 1932), p. 197, (who argues to retain the absolute aspect); and A. D'Arbo, *The Decline of Mechanics*, pp. 106-114.

39. Boltzmann, identifying the increase in entropy with the passage from a less probable to a more probable state, equated this transition with the "flow of time." Thus physical time was interpreted by him in terms of past and future—past, as a less probable, and future, as a more probable state of the universe. Proceeding from Boltzmann's introduction of directed time into physics, Eddington further introduces the concept of becoming into the physical world. According to him, the second law of Thermodynamics, which makes reversibility impossible, gives a dynamic one-way property to reality. Time is no longer static but presents a flowing movement, and, although becoming is a qualitative phenomenon having no place in the numerical code of entropy, it still exists even in the world of the physicist. The passage from Boltzmann's mechanistic formulation of entropy to metaphysical metamorphosis in a qualitative world is, Eddington maintains, necessary and quite simple.

"It is so welded into our consciousness that a moving on of time is a condition of consciousness. We have direct insight into "becoming" which sweeps aside all usual symbolic knowledge as on an inferior plane. If I grasp the notion or existence because I myself exist, I grasp the notion of becoming because I myself become. It is the innermost Ego of all which is and which becomes."

The echo of Bergson's voice in his "debate" with the Astronomer Royal (Chapter 3) is audible. The philosopher here supplants the physicist. Eddington, *The Nature of the Physical World*, p. iv,v. V. Bergson, *L'evolution Creatrice*; F. Auerbach, *Die Welt Herrin und ihr Schattan*; W. Stern, *Person und Sache*; M. Scheler, *Vom Ewigen in Menschen*, (Berlin: 1933), pp. 508-510; M. Planck, *The Philosophy of Physics*, Part III ("Scientific Ideas"); A. D'Abro, *op. cit.*, p. 419-420; P.W. Bridgman, *The Logic of Modern Physics*.

40. James never reconciled the sensationist psychologist with the

author of purposive psychology in himself. V. Wm. McDougall. *Outline of Psychology*, Preface pp. v-xii; pp. 1-42.

41. Wm. James. *Pluralistic Universe*, "On the Continuity of Experience."

42. H. Bergson, *Introduction to Metaphysics*, p. 9.

43. Reality as "becoming" is one of the most salient features of James and Dewey's philosophies. They speak of a world in the making. However, the *actus*-character of reality is to be understood from a pragmatic viewpoint exclusively. "Becoming" as a metaphysical ideal emerges in Whitehead's philosophy.

44. Nietzche's Dionysian instinctive wisdom vs. conceptual Socratism is similar to the conflict of the mathematico-scientific and humanistic methodologies. See *The Birth of Tragedy*, chap. XIII.

45. The Spinozistic conception of substance compared to that of the scientist serves as a conspicuous illustration of the methodological distinction between the physical and metaphysical methods. Both postulate substance as demonstrated in its attribute of extension, but while Spinoza derives the particular or infinitesimal from the infinite substance and its attributes, the scientist moves in the opposite direction. Beginning with "infinitesimal" units, he constructs an infinite substance (matter).

Spinoza, moving from the infinite to the infinitesimal, constructed a most magnificent system of metaphysics. The scientist, proceeding from the simplest unit to the cosmic process, never attempts to draw any metaphysical conclusions or collide with the Absolute; but develops a complex functional system of mathematical interdependencies. Movement from the infinitesimal to the infinite results in science. Both the humanistic sciences and modern philosophy apply the Spinozistic method in new forms.

46. When Rabad criticized Maimonides for including the non-corporeality of God among his articles of faith, he was guided by the practical needs of the worshipper who imagines God in sensible forms. V. Maimonidean *Code*, *Teshuvah*, III, 7, and Rabad's comments.

47. "The experiences we have been studying...plainly show the universe to be a more many-sided affair than any sect, even the scientific sect, allows for...the obvious outcome of our total experience is that the world can be handled according to many systems of ideas, and is so handled by different men, and will each time give some characteristic type of profit. ... Evidently, then, the science and the religion are the both of them genuine keys for unlocking the

world's treasure house…and why after all may not the world be so complex as to consist of many interpreting spheres of reality, which we can thus approach in alternatives by using different attitudes…" Wm. James, *Varieties of Religious Experience*, pp. 120-121.

48. This calls to mind the scholastic idea of *vis aestimativa*, of the practical cognitive assignment given by Descartes to the perceptions conditioning our emotional life; and of Lotze's theory that emotions involving pain and pleasure are cognitive apprehensions of values. In its modern form the concept of intentionality was formulated by Brentano, Husserl, Scheler and Hartmann.

49. Hume denied the intentional character of our emotional experiences: "A passion is an original existence, or, if you will, modification of existence; and contains not any representative quality which renders it a copy of any other existence or modification. When I am angry, I am actually possessed with the passion, and in that emotion have no more a reference to any other object, than when I am thirsty, or sick or more than five feet high." *Treatise of Human Nature*. Part III, section iii.

John Dewey, whose viewpoint regarding the problem of intentionality is synonymous with that of Hume, distinguishes between the "direct, active, non-cognitive experience of goods and bads and that of valuation, the latter being simply the mode of judgment like any other form of judgment." This attitude is in consonance with Dewey's pragmatic theory of the non-reflectional practical temperament of the true "theoretician." However, the cognitive operation of "appraising" and "estimating" (in contradistinction to "prizing" and "esteeming" which are non-cognitive) is an essential component of the religious act. Hence the intellectual gesture is characteristic of the *homo-religiosus*. V. John Dewey, *Essays in Experimental Logic*, (Chicago: 1916).

50. The scope of this essay does not permit investigating the concept of cognitive intentionality. Brentano, the father of the intentional act, denied its cognitive character and conceived intentionality as non-cognitive directedness upon an object. Husserl and Scheler, however, discovered cognitive layers within the structural whole of intentional experience. Scheler, in particular, developed the thesis that our sentiments are inexhaustible treasures of sympathetic apprehension of the pure eternal essences.

51. The connative character—which is a commonplace of psychology—of our emotional experience is the psychological counterpart to epistemological intentionality. The emotional qualities endowed

with an impulsive power are directed upon objects and imply cognitive functions. And though psychologists still hold that emotions "signify to us primarily not the nature of things, but rather the nature of our impulsive reaction to things," epistemologists and metaphysicians think differently nonetheless and are bent on isolating an objective cognitive function. Philosophers are intrigued especially by the cognitive aspect of emotional experience as they proceed from emotion to sentiment ("an organized system of dispositions"). The latter is surely associated with an objective cognitive operation. Cf. James' *Principles of Psychology*, chapter on "The Stream of Thought," section on 'Feelings of Tendency'; also his chapter on "Will," in which he expounds the view that "effort of attention is the essential phenomenon of will," and that "consent to the idea's individual presence is that effort's sole achievement." V. William McDougall, *Outline of Psychology*, chaps. XI, XVI. John H. Muirhead, *The Platonic Tradition in Anglo-Saxon Philosophy*. pp. 67, 69, 367.

52. Neo-Hegelian metaphysicians, substituting experience for thought, rehabilitated the will and the sentiments and assigned to *them* cognitive functions.

53. This illustration is in consonance with the attitude adopted by Malebranche according to which a value-judgment precedes the act of love. Modern epistemology seems to doubt the veracity of this thesis. N. Malebranche, *Recherche de la Verité*. vol. II; H. Bluhr, *Religioese Erotik*; M. Scheler, *Wesen und Formen der Sympathie*.

54. The cognitive background of the volitional and affective life was known to Kant, who called his ethics *Critique of Practical Reason* and his aesthetics *Critique of Judgment*.

55. The idea of autonomous religious knowledge may be traced to medieval Arabic and Christian scholasticism. The theory or twofold truth attributed to Averroës (Ibn Roshd) and developed by Duns Scotus in his *"Reportata Parisiana"* and by Petrus Pompanatius in his *"Tractatus de Immortabilitate Animae"*; and further cultivated by the philosophers of the Renaissance (as a shield against the persecution by the Church), proclaimed the paradoxical maxim that what is false in science may be true in religion and vice-versa. The modern concept of the duality of religious and scientific knowledge differs from the above-mentioned scholastic theory in two main points: First, while the theory of two-fold truth referred mainly to single scientific and religious propositions, modern philosophy avoids as many controversial issues as possible with regard to specific scientific state-

ments. It is bent solely upon methodological pluralism with all its ramifications extending into the metaphysical and speculative.

Second, current pluralism does not speak of truth and falsity as the medievalists did. The scholastic dictum, "what is true in religion may be false in science," is nonsensical according to our modern viewpoint. Rather than incline to a perspective that the religious and scientific aspects negate and contradict, we prefer to accept many complementary approaches to reality.

56. The idea that the religious act is endowed with cognitive features distinct from the rationalistic approach to reality is already latent in the doctrine of fideism that divorces religion from metaphysics. The father of fideism, Augustine, with his famous dictum *"in lumen Dei omnia cogniscimus"* (that Thomas Aquinas converted into *"per lumen Dei"*), equated knowledge of the intelligible world with illumination and immediate revelation. Yehuda Halevi's "invisible and eternal eye" that apprehends supersensible things likewise denotes a different sources of religious cognitive experience. Mystics, pantheistic as well as practical, claimed to draw knowledge of the transcendental from such unique sources. These undercurrents of occidental religious thought flowed into Luther's individualism and the pietistic faith philosophy. Both led to subjectivistic prodigality in interpreting the religious act. Max Scheler, *Vom Ewigen im Menschen*, p. 433; W. Windelband, *History of Philosophy*; *Religious Realism*, ed. by D. C. Mackintosh, chap. 10; E. W. Lyman, *Can Religious Intuition Give Knowledge of Reality?* And see *Kuzari*, IV, 3.

57. The original intent of Ritschlian philosophy was to separate religion completely from the ontological domain, assigning to it an axiological function only. In its more advanced stages, however, religious axiology reverted to ontology.

58. The reason for this overzealous search for finality, so popular among contemporary theologians, is the passionate desire of every philosopher of religion to legitimate the cognitive validity and truthfulness of religious propositions. Yet the problem of evidence in religion will never be solved. The believer does not miss philosophic legitimation; the skeptic will never be satisfied with any cognitive demonstration. This ticklish problem became the Gordian knot of many theological endeavors. Philosophers of religion would have achieved more had they dedicated themselves to the task of interpreting concrete reality in terms and concepts that fit into the framework of a religious world perspective.

59. Hegel's philosophy of religion, envisaging in the latter the culmination of learning, art and all other cultural accomplishments, is a grand attempt at interpreting religion from a cognitive standpoint. Yet, Hegel ignored both scientific and religious realities.

60. "As regards the second request, [Moses] was told 'Thou canst not see My Face.' The words, 'all My goodness' imply that God promised to show him the whole creation concerning what is stated, 'And God saw all He created and behold it was very good.' And when I say He showed him the whole creation, God promised to make him comprehend the nature of things, their relation to each other and the way they are governed by God both in reference to the universe as a whole and to each creature in particular." *The Guide of the Perplexed*, I, 54 (Friedlander's translation).

61. The frequent collisions of the church and positive science will confirm our thesis that there are cognitive trends in the world of religion and that the *homo religiosus* is concerned with the sensible universe reality. It would be absurd to maintain that the interference of organized religion with scientific advancement was prompted by political or practical motives alone. The conflict arose rather from the essential cognitive interests of a religion challenged by science. The controversy did not rage so much about single scientific propositions as it did about an entire world perspective which was incommensurable with the basic religious cognitive outlook. Religion could not (and will not) recognize the scientifically postulated universe as its own.

Moreover, aside from all historical considerations, cognitive tendencies are to be discerned in the unshakable feeling of certainty accompanying the religious experience. We know that the *homo religiosus* claims the highest degree of truth for the objects coordinated with his beliefs. Indeed, in many instances this surpasses in intensity, clarity and certainty the truth-awareness of the scientist. In some cases the *homo religiosus* is so overwhelmed by the impact of his experience that he very distinctly perceives the reality of his object. He is fully conscious of the existence of the transcendental order. If the religious object be real, the worshipper is impelled to interpret it, and the interpretation is always in terms of an autonomous method.

Otto, although ingenious in his analysis of the numinous character of the religious experience, does not do it full justice in stating that the *mysterium tremendum* which confronts the *homo religiosus* exhausts itself in arousing a feeling of awe and dread. On the contrary, the religious *numen* does not only stimulate the *homo religiosus* to an emotional state or awe, but also arouses in him a passion for cognition of the incomprehensible. He is both fascinated and repelled—fascinated by the *mysterium magnum*; repelled by the *mysterium tremendum*. Moses sees the burning bush. On the one hand, confronted by the *mysterium tremendum*, he hides his face in fear of looking upon God; but, on the other hand, he says, "I will turn aside now and I will see this great sight as to why the bush is not consumed." The *homo religiosus* senses the insolubility of the mystery but nonetheless yields to an irresistible temptation to solve it.

The religious act *is* ambivalent and fraught with paradox. Isolating the numinous component from the complex of the religious act and construing it as its basis, Otto inevitably must regard any metaphysical urge as alien to the *homo religiosus*. He sees the basic religious experience not as an all-enveloping act, but as an act directed exclusively upon the absolute transcendence and otherness of God. It is self evident that, if the religious experience be reduced to a non-rational and ineffable aspect, cognitive components are precluded, for the transcendental is incomprehensible. V. William James, *Varieties of Religious Experience*, Lecture 3 ("The Reality of the Unseen"); E. Cassirer, *Essay on Man*, pp. 85-86; Rudolf Otto, *The Idea of the Holy*.

62. One of the foremost proponents of an autonomous religious knowledge and of an unique epistemology of religion was Max Scheler, to whose *Vom Ewigen im Menschen* this work is indebted in several important points. Yet Scheler's philosophic temperament, his passionate metaphysical yearning for the ontological and axiological Absolute, and his emotional sweep eclipsed his clear vision, and led him, in many instances, to arbitrary conclusions. The main defect in Scheler's mother discipline of religion, Eidology (with its ancillary disciplines of epistemology, axiology and the metaphysics of religion), is that it moves in a vacuum. There is no objective order underlying his eidology of religion. Furthermore, his unique religious categories refer mainly to the hypersensible world. Concrete reality is left to metaphysics. Like the Christian gnostic of old, Scheler craves for *gnosis* of the divine. His religious knowledge ignores the "here and now" reality.

63. Cf. the Newtonian differentiation of absolute and relative time; also the controversy between Aristotle and Plotinus regarding the priority of motion and time. The religious viewpoint is more in harmony with the Aristotelian thesis that motion generates time.

64. Cf. Leibnitz' maxim: *Le present est chargé du passé, et gros de l'avenir*; also Whitehead's "prejudice of simple locations."

65. Anti-intellectualistic tendencies are not new in philosophy. Parallel to the main stream of rationalistic occidental thought, there has always swirled a peculiar anti-intellectualistic undercurrent. From time to time it has broken through the dam of critical human reasoning and taken form in non-rational postulates and principles. The background of such "insurgent" philosophical movements has always been skepticism. However, we must discriminate between two forms of skepticism: positivistic and idealistic. While the positivistic and skeptical temperament is a healthy phenomenon and has a sobering effect upon philosophical thought, idealistic skepticism may under certain circumstances intoxicate the human mind and adumbrate mysticism. This dichotomy is best illustrated by the ancient Greek skeptical mood, on the one hand, and by Kantian transcendental skepticism, on the other. The philosophic doubt that stimulated the nominalistic and positivistic schools throughout the ages has, today, challenged the ultimate grounds and absolute validity of scientific knowledge. In such manner it has stimulated human thinking. It has broken down dogmatic barriers and cleared the philosophic path of the debris of obsolete traditionalism. Kant himself confessed that Hume "awoke him from him dogmatic slumber."

The situation changes, however, as soon as reality is bifurcated and skepticism joined with apriorism, as was the case with Kantian philosophy. The Kantian dualistic approach to reality, ascribing validity and universality to certain scientific propositions of phenomenal nature while, concomitantly, confessing ignorance in the realm of the Absolute, led to speculative thought replete with philosophic anomalies. If there be a mysterious "thing in itself," however unintelligible it prove, the philosopher is challenged to grasp it. Speculative philosophy was born the very moment Kant discovered the incomprehensible "Thing in itself." Schelling's artistic intuition, Schopenhauer's voluntaristic metaphysics, Hegel's excessive idealism and contemporary metaphysics of the Absolute, from Bradley to Max Scheler and Hartmann, are characteristic of the daring mood of the philosopher who undertakes to solve the insoluble. The net results of these metaphysical acrobatics were philosophic confusion and logical bewilderment. Scientific skepticism is a blessing while transcendental skepticism very often leads to metaphysical perplexities and mysticism.

66. V. Nietzsche, *Ecce Homo*, chap. 4; also *The Birth of Tragedy*, chap.

20. See also W. Dannhouser's study, *Nietzsche's Image of Socrates*.

67. Kretschmer, *Koerperbau und Charakter*; Reininger, *Das Psychophysiche Problem*; Walter Del Negro, "Das Strukturproblem in der Philosophie der Gegenwart," *Kant Studien*, 1932, Vol. XXXVII.

68. "Whatness," although ignored by the explanatory disciplines of physics and chemistry, is still a very important aspect of the descriptive sciences such as general botany (particularly taxonomy and plant morphology) and zoology. The qualitative "what" and not the quantitative "how" determines the methodical description of genera and species. Qualitative appearance is the main concern of the descriptive sciences. Even explanatory chemistry is pervaded with a semi-qualitative spirit.

Similarly the problem of concrete individuality (in contra-distinction to the abstract universal) emerges in the natural sciences. Descriptive disciplines like geography and geology, instead of dealing with genera and species, study unique and crude individualities. They operate not only with conceptual abstractions in Platonic and Aristotelian fashion, but also with geographical and geological "living" configurations with all their singularities. A geographical zone or a geological epoch is not a universal but an individual structure. We do not require the geographer or geologist to present the common and general aspects of his subject and so enable us to reduce the latter to already known elements which are commensurable with other conceptual orders. We expect him to expose the ramifications of the unique and individual and to give a physiognomical interpretation of his subject. The geographer, like the historian, is in some respects an artist creating "living" forms. The epistemological problems associated with the method of individual abstraction emerge, not only in history (the problem child of philosophy since Aristotle), but also in the natural descriptive sciences. A little magnanimity in interpreting the term "science" is to be recommended. The descriptive method is autonomous and scientific. There is no reason for equating the scientific method with causalistic explanation. Cf. Heinrich Rickert, *Die Grenzen der Naturwissenschaftenlichen Begriffsbildung* (Tuebingen and Leipzig: 1902), p. 235; Ernst Cassirer, *Substanzbegriff und Funktionsbegriff.* (Berlin: 1910), pp. 292-310. Heinrich Maier, *Das Historische Erkennen* (Goettingen: 1914), and *Wahrheit und Wirklichkeit* (Tuebingen: 1926), pp. 461-466, 561.

69. Biology deals also with the same problem. We have shown above that the Bergsonian revolt against the tyranny of the mathemat-

ical science gained impetus with the vitalistic trends rampant in biology since Darwin and Lamarck's evolutionism. Although there is still no unanimity among students of biology and physiology as to the interpretation of the phenomenon of life (so that Bergson's enthusiasm was a little premature), one fact is nonetheless clear: the problem of the living Gestalt is central in the sciences of life. Even the mechanists have to cope with the problem of the "whole."

70. "We are accustomed to consider the universe as made up of parts, and mathematicians usually begin by considering a certain particle, and then conceiving its relation to another particle, and so on. This has generally been supposed the most general method. To conceive of a particle, however, requires a process of abstraction, since all our perceptions are related to extended bodies, so that the idea of a whole that is in our consciousness at a given instant is perhaps as primitive an idea as that of any individual thing. Hence there may be a mathematical method in which we proceed from the whole to the parts instead or from the parts to the whole." Clerk Maxwell, *Electricity and Magnetism* (Oxford: 1982), vol. XI, p. 176-177.

Maxwell's methodological innovation, however, remained unnoticed until Gestalt theory made headway in psychology and pervaded the sciences of life–biology and physiology. Psychology, looking for a physiological counterpart to the higher psychical structures, and anxious to avoid any collision with the biological mechanist, finally turned to physics for structural design.

The first attempt was made by Koehler, who, primarily interested in the physiologico-psychological aspect, started investigations in the field of electricity. According to him, electrical magnitudes like charge, field, electrostatic energy and current display structural patterns. He even extended the Gestalt character to other forms of energy. Although these magnitudes, being expressed by the principle of the conservation of energy, are of a summative nature, they nevertheless assume structural appearance in their spatial manifestations. Energy in its entirety presents, using the Aristotelian metaphor, the "hyletic matter" which is crystallized by physical topography into concrete spatial configurations. Charge, electro-static energy, current, etc., despite their additive character, are forced by physical topography into the framework of the whole. As topographic magnitudes, they meet the two requirements formulated by Ehrenfels in reference to Gestalt qualities.

In view of the fact that spatial topography (which in most cases can be reduced to optical and tactual properties) is the determining agent of physical structures, physical Gestalt unity applies only to finite, concrete and disparate systems. Since the physical process itself is of an additive nature (it is only its revelation through physical topography that displays structural characteristics), no cosmological metaphysical implications are associated with the concept of Gestalt. The cosmos as a whole, its causality and "substance," remains, as ever, an end-product of piecemeal summations. Such a theory is perhaps of great importance to the psychologist who looks for physical counterparts to the structural aspects of the consciousness, but it is of no relevance to the philosopher and metaphysician. The field equations expressing structural laws, however, do not fit into the scheme of physical concrete topography and separability. Koehler himself was aware that his physical structures are not in consonance with Maxwell's attempt to place exclusive value upon the properties of the field and to account for the concrete electrically charged conductor in terms of field magnitudes. If the charge be reduced to a mathematical fiction, then it is nonsensical to speak of topography. Koehler, however, tried to solve this difficulty by refusing to accept a pure field theory. He subscribed to Lorentz' electron-field theory that presupposes both a continuous non-mechanical field and matter which is represented by electrons and protons governed by mechanical laws. In such manner he thought it possible to introduce concrete topography into the field. The charged conductor and the field emerge side by side as two physical realities.

("Zu einer gegebenen form, welcher Lodung zugefuehrt ist, gehoert eine Eigenstruktur der Energie im umgebenden Felde.") It is obvious that such a solution does not entirely eliminate the difficulty. The limiting of the Gestalt aspect to non-existent quasi-isolated systems enveloped by concrete finitude collides with the field magnitude which has no physical topography and which theoretically extends to infinity. If such physical structures do not correspond to the original electromagnetic field magnitudes, it is still more difficult to reconcile them with the gravitational (metrical) equations of relativity which are again structural laws. The fact that the gravitational field has not yet been successfully formulated as a pure field, and that the atomicity of matter is still an experimental reality does not alter the problem. W. Koehler, *Die Physischen Gestalten*, pp. 75, 78, 79, 153, 161.

71. Owing to the abstract and symbolic character of the microscopic

magnitudes with which quantum mechanics operate, the aspect of the whole refers more to mathematical equivalents than to actual concreteness and Gestalt contours. This is consonant with Maxwell's original thought regarding a dualistic mathematical approach, the summative and the structural. This dualism is not ascribable to the discrepancy existing between the mathematician (who *in abstracto* dissociates and integrates) and the physicist (who is equipped with a unique sense for envisaging the "real dynamical"), but to mathematical symbolism itself.

72. "Modern physics has given us a clear indication pointing in the same direction. It has taught us that the nature of any system cannot be discovered by dividing it into its component parts and studying each part by itself since such a method often implies the loss of the important properties of the system. We must keep our attention fixed on the whole and on the interconnection between the parts. The same is true of our intellectual life. It is impossible to make a clear cut between science, religion and art. The whole is never equal simply to the sum of its various parts." Max Planck, *The Philosophy of Physics*, pp. 34-35. See also A. Einstein, *The Evolution of Physics*, pp. 148-149; J.E. Boodin, "Russell's Metaphysics," in *The Library of Living Philosophers*, vol. V, pp. 489, 507, 508.

73. In an interesting article, "*Die Erfassung der Quantengesetze durch kontinuierliche Funktionen*" (*Naturwissenschaften*, June 1929), Schroedinger elaborates upon the part played by the concept of the whole in modern physics.

After Planck introduced his quantum hypothesis, attempts were made to fit it into the framework of the classical theory, but the gap became even wider as time went on. While classical physics was essentially free of discontinuities in the spatio-temporal classification of phenomena, and in principle, given the boundary conditions, it was possible to specify exactly what is happening to any point at any time, no such description could be obtained of the Rutherford-Bohr atom; the theoretical results flatly contradicted the experiment. Wave mechanics made possible a return to a method which somehow resembles the classical description. At least, continuous functions (i.e., the probability wave function) of temporal and spatial coordinates reappear, such as the function (e.g., potential) in electromagnetic theory; and, as in that theory, partial differential equations dominate the mathematics of the field. However, integrals or quadratures of these functions are the quantities with physical significance. They are analogous to the Fourier coefficients discussed above. Hence, in quantum physics the photochemical effect is a property of the wave as a whole and not something arising from successive contributions of separate parts. A similar interpretation is to be put on a ψ function. A ψ function is not to be thought of as describing a system piecemeal by summing the whole of individual points of the system, but rather as determining the observable behavior of the system through the form of the ψ function.

Schroedinger stresses the point that, whereas the particular "Eigenfunctions" of classical physics are essentially reflections of boundary conditions (controlled by experiments) and the Gestalt qualities are of arbitrary and contingent character (he refers to Koehler's "Physische Gestalten"), in quantum mechanics they are determined by nature. The Gestalt property is inherent in the mathematical function itself and constitutes the very essence of the physical process. "The method in the quantum theory opens to us vistas of 'Gestalt' which are of direct importance for the understanding of nature. ... The Eigenfunctions of atoms and molecules depend no more on contingent and arbitrary factors; they are determined by nature. The Eigenfuctions are actually the decisive Gestalt elements of the observable occurrence."

74. Whittaker, *Philosophical Magazine and Journal of Science*, London, April 1943. Also H. Weyl, *An Open World*.

75. Vide Paul Natorp, *Allgemeine Psychologie nach Kritischer Methode* (Tuebingen: 1912). I am indebted to this book in several important points.

76. That mathematics is not synonymous with receptive intuition, as Kant thought, was amply demonstrated by modern mathematics. It is sufficient to consider the Weierstrass curve in order to convince oneself of the incommensurability of mathematical knowledge with "sensuous" intuition. The development of non-Euclidean geometry refuted Kant's "Transcendental Aesthetics" completely.

77. This conversion is not to be understood from a genetic viewpoint. It expresses rather a systematic, functional process.

78. The concept of self-transcendence finds its echo in Kant's introduction of God, Universe, and soul as regulative ideas of the theoretical reason, which allude to horizons far beyond the cognitive domain. Fichte's universal non-ego, Hegel's idea of otherness within the ontological panlogistic monistic process, and particularly the Neo-Kantian eternal task (*Aufgabe*) that lies beyond the realm of fulfill-

ment and Bradley's idea of the Absolute that is conceived but not realized by the reason–all these reflect the act of self-transcendence on the part of the logos and ethos. The psychological theory of interaction of mind and body (*influxus physicus*) is also based upon self-transcendence.

79. These phenomena are, again objectified data of something more subjective and inaccessible. Pure subjectivity is a fiction similar to Aristotelian pure matter.

80. In contrast with Kantian ethics, the Jewish viewpoint gives priority to the outward act and the realization of the norm in the physical realm. The motivation plays a minor role and the decision   · itself is of secondary importance.

81. Of course, it is paradoxical to speak of causality–an instrument of objectification–in the subjective region. However, since no ideal of pure subjectivity exists, we may perhaps introduce some relational principle in that sphere. But again the objective aspect is immune to causal determination. An antinomy of enormous magnitude is linked with the concept of causality in the internal world. The ancient dichotomy of freedom and determinism is nurtured on the paradoxical character of objectivity which rests upon subjective premises.

82. To avoid misunderstanding, it must be stressed that subjectivity be not misconceived as something figmentary. It has the same ontological character as objectivity. On the contrary, the history of philosophy will attest that many thinkers regarded subjectivity as the primary aspect of which we are ontologically conscious. Descartes' "cogito" is nothing more than an affirmation of his faith in the inward world. Doubting the existence of everything external, he still did not dare to cast the aspersion of skepticism upon his ego. Starting from inwardness, he then rediscovered the existence of an external world. Many idealistic theories that coordinate existence with thinking begin with a similar thesis. Spiritual reality is superior to physical, and participates in the constitution of the latter. Of course, there are exceptions, and advanced idealistic doctrines did not differentiate between the physical and the psychical. Adopting Kant's concept of pure reason which denotes a non-existent psychical ideal process of cognition, idealism permits such a free agent to constitute reality in its entirety, physis and psyche. However, since Berkeley, classical idealism cultivated the naive Cartesian faith in the certitude of the existence of the ego. Inward life was considered as something immediate and absolute, with which the "logos" is intimately acquainted. The

ontological experience of selfhood is not acquired, according to those theories, in a reflective mood, but is immediately apprehended. Subject and object merge; "cogito" and "sum" converge. The subjective world which strikes us with its full impingement appeared, to the idealist of old, of a higher order than external reality.

83. Vide Paul Natorp, *op. cit.*

84. Even one of the founders of the Neo-Kantian school, Paul Natorp, adopted a similar attitude towards religion. It is interesting to observe one of the apostles of scientific philosophy proclaiming religion to be pure subjectivity. This tendency was ascribable to the fact that the scientific method was considered omnipotent and its approach to reality monistic and exclusive. Religion was at great odds in its attempt to gain cognitive access to the world. While Kant tried to relegate religion to the ethical sphere, thus stripping it of any cognitive vestige, Natorp, placing religion within humanity, declared it as *toto generi* different from science. In contrast with science, religion, he said, expresses the subjective attitude of man when confronted with reality.

85. Schleiermacher, *Reden ueber Religion*.

86. S. Kierkegaard, *Concluding Unscientific Postscript*, pp. 116-21. Kierkegaard himself as a *homo religiosus* was in continuous strife with his contemporary world. He spoke of a divine madness by which the religionist is obsessed, and which brings him into collision with the secular order of things. V. *Fear and Trembling* and *Repetition*.

87. The more conservative representatives of religious subjectivism like Schleiermacher (as a professional theologian) and Sabatier, know of a passage from emotional subjectivity to the objective historical. Schleiermacher, for instance, endeavors to demonstrate how the immediate consciousness passes into external objective forms. Theology, in line with his thought, borrows symbols from philosophy in order to express certain phases of the inner religious life. Historians agree that such philosophic efforts met with complete failure. Schleiermacher, *Glaubenslehre*; A. Sabatier, *Outlines of a Philosophy of Religion*.

88. Although knowledge is an important factor in the religious act, it still serves a normative end. The approach of the *homo religiosus* is not purely theoretical. His guiding motif is the norm that ultimately leads him to a cognitive act. The norm precedes, the act of cognition follows.

89. V. Anatole France, *Thais*.

90. As a matter of fact, the monastery and the nunnery denote more anti-hedonic than anti-social tendencies. Their members sever affiliation with the world indulged in pleasure, not with the world at large. As for the Jewish religion, the concept of congregation— צבור —is a central them in Halakhah. Many laws refer directly to the collective and not to the individual. The צבור is a recipient of a religious norm.

91. George Malcolm Stratton, *Psychology of the Religious Life* (London and New York: 1918), chap. 11; Emile Boutroux, *Science and Religion*, chap. IV, 2; Max Scheler, *Vom Ewigen im Menschen* (Berlin: 1933), pp. 553-558.

92. The sociological approach, in this respect, is superior to the psychological. See E. Boutroux, *Religion and Science*; Emil Brunner, *The Philosophy of Religion*, p. 26; Karl Barth, *Die Lehrer vom Worte Gottes*, Dogmatic I.

93. The movement of religious realism, here and abroad, is a natural reaction to the anthropocentric subjectivistic interpretation of the religious act that dominated philosophic thought of the 19th century. Religious realism, while attempting to construct objective criteria, and extending the religious act into the external world, overlooked the uniqueness of the religious norm and confused it with ethical or aesthetic attitudes. V. H. R. Niebuhr, *Religious Realism in the 20th Century*, pp. 413-432; D.C. Mackintosh, *op. cit.*; Paul Tillich, *Religioese Lage der Gegenwart*; *Religioese Verwirklichung*.

A powerful movement to divorce religion from subjectivism and romanticism was initiated by Karl Barth and his associates. Unfortunately their "theology of crisis" plunges into religious agnosticism and skepticism, and denudes faith of its psychical components. According to Barthian theology, faith (in contradistinction to religion) is intrinisically non-cognitive and non-cultural. v. Brunner, *Religionsphilosophie Evangelischer Theologie*, (Muenchen: 1929); Brunner, *Erlebnis, Erkenntnis und Glaube*; K. Barth, *Die Lehre vom Worte Gottes*.

94. As aforementioned, the psychologist must avail himself of the method of reconstruction if causal interpretation is not to be precluded. The only difference between the psychologist and the philosopher is that, while the psychologist, guided by the "how" question, coordinates subjective religious aspects with those of the mundane cultural consciousness, the philosopher, searching for the "what," limits his investigation to the religious domain and explores objective forms only in retrospect.

95. Edmund Husserl, *Logische Untersuchungen*, vol. I; H. Maier, *Wahrheit und Wirklichkeit*, vol. I, Introduction.

96. William James, in his first lecture on religion and neurology (in *Varieties of Religious Experience*), divorced completely the *homo religiosus* from the neurological type and proclaimed that "immediate luminousness, philosophic reasonableness and moral helpfulness are the only available criteria" for the religious act.

97. Such a diety is neither new nor useful. The ancient Greek philosophers knew of the *logos* and the *nous* which were by far more fascinating than the modern Universe-God; and still these deities surrendered to the personal God of the apocalypse.

The liberals begin with certain speculative premises and portray an imaginary divinity. They completely ignore the practical religious needs of man and try to impose upon him a God for whom he has neither love nor fear. It has often proven to be the case that a purely pantheistic Ethos-Divinity has no appeal to the average worshipper. The idea of God reduced to a cosmic moral force is devoid of meaning.

98. The problem of change and metamorphosis in religious life is one of the most complicated in the philosophy of religion. The Halakhah distinguishes between חידוש and שינוי. For a discussion of this distinction and of this problem, see my Hebrew article, ובקשתם משם.

99. See Saadiah, *Emunot ve'Deot*, III, sections 1-3; and Bahya ibn Pakuda *Hovot Ha'Levavot*, III, section 5.

100. Saadiah's causal approach is found in III, 2.

101. A similar theory of religious instrumentalism was developed by Kant in his philosophy of religion. Kant justifies worship and formal service as symbolic of inner religiosity. He ascribes, however, secondary value to the concrete, psychological religious act. It serves only as a means to a higher end. Formal service cultivates and promotes man's ethical endeavor which alone is the core of the religious personality. See *Die Religion Innerhalb der Grenzen der Vernunft.*

102. אף על פי שתקיעת שופר בראש השנה גזירת הכתוב רמז יש בו כלומר עורו ישנים משנתכם ונרדמים הקיצו מתרדמתכם וחפשו במעשיכם וחזרו בתשובה וזכרו בוראכם.

103. *Avudraham*, Prague edition, III, 4. Of course, we may always interpret Saadiah's ten reasons for the sounding of the shofar in a purely symbolic sense.

104. דבר ברור וגלוי שהטומאות והטהרות גזירות הכתוב הן ואינן מדברים
שדעתו של אדם מכרעתו והרי הן מכלל החוקים. וכן הטבילה מן הטומאות מכלל
החוקים היא שאין הטומאה טיט או צואה שתעבור במים אלא גזירת הכתוב
היא והדבר תלוי בכוונת הלב.

105. Cf. Saadiah, *op. cit.* Also *Kuzari*, III, 5.

106. אמנם ענין השבת טעמו מפורסם ואין צריך לביאור כבר נודע מה שבו
מהמנוחה עד שיהיה שביעית חיי אדם בהנאה ובמנוחה מהעמל והטורח שלא ימלט ממנו
קטן וגדול עם מה שמתמיד ומקיים הבעת הנכבד מאד לדורות והיא האמונה בחדוש
העולם. See also II, 31, where Maimonides discusses the double biblical
reasons for the observance of Sabbath: creation and redemption.
Both, however, are of a symbolic nature. The words ותיקון העניׇ הגשמי
refer to the commemoration of the exodus from Egypt. See the
comments of *Efodi* and Abravanel on the relevant passages of the
*Guide*.

107. *Mishneh Torah*, Laws of Sabbath, XXX, 15.

108. The controversy between Maimonides and Nachmandies in
reference to the interpretation of sacrifice is characteristic of the
contrast prevailing between the causalistic and retrospective reconstruction methods.

In the *Guide*, Maimonides sees in sacrifice just an educational
method of elevating the Jew above such forms of worship. Previously,
sacrifice had been the common practice of the heathens among whom
the Jews had lived. In order to direct the Jew towards worship of
God, the Torah made the concession of animal sacrifice. Nachmanides
severely criticizes Maimonides for his rationalization, and introduced
his own interpretation. Sacrifice, for him, refers actually to man himself. Worship is nothing but mental sacrifice. And animal sacrifice
symbolizes the internal act of self-negation.

Whatever the merit of Nachmanides' interpretation, one thing is
clear. Philosophically it is far superior to Maimonides' explanation.
While Maimonides' causalistic aspect in the *Guide* is pure instrumentalism, Nachmanides' interpretation penetrates the complex concept
of sacrifice itself. He has elaborated an idea which may have some
modern philosophical merit. v. *Guide* III, 45-46. See also
Nachmanides, Commentary on Leviticus, I, 9; v. quotation above in
*Code, Me'ila*, VIII, 8.

109. C. G. Jung's interpretation of the religious act as a symbolic
surrogate for a "libido accumulation" serves as an example of the
causalistic approach to religion. The regressive movement of this
libido towards the primordial does not describe the religious experi-

ence but annuls it. His regression is nothing but a causal explanatory method that supplants religion with a magnitude more obscure and mysterious than the transcendent and supernatural. The differentiation between sign and symbol is of no help towards the understanding of the religious act. Whether we reduce the sign to a known, or a symbol to an unknown phenomenon is irrelevant. Both explain but do not describe. Freud's interpretation of God as a Father surrogate is again typical of the causalistic fallacy. In general, the negating and destructive force of genetics reaches its high-point in the psychoanalytic interpretation of spiritual phenomena. V. C. Turg, *Psychological Types*, (London: 1923), pp. 157-8; 601. See also Arthur Hazard Dakin, *Man the Measure*, chap. 4.

110. In contrast with subsumptive logic, modern philosophy considers the traditional Aristotelian or Kantian categories as dynamic, constantly changing methods, rather than rigid notions forming the apex of a conceptual hierarchy. The *fieri-* character of cognition is a commonplace of contemporary epistemology. The categorical flux can only be discovered in the subjective sphere.

# INDEX*

Abravanel, I., 131n
Aquinas, Thomas, 73, 118n
Aristotle, 5, 6, 32, 41, 57, 75-9,
  90, 93, 105n, 106n, 107n, 109n,
  120n, 122n, 123n, 132n
Auerbach, F., 114n
Augustine, 118n
Avenarius, R., 11, 12
Averroës, 117n
*Avudraham*, 130n

Bahya ibn Pakuda, 92, 130n
Barth, K., 3, 129n
Bergson, H., 8, 9, 13, 14, 20, 29,
  31, 33-35, 47, 53, 109n, 113n,
  114n, 115n, 122n
Berkeley, G., 106n, 107n, 127n
Bluhr, H., 117n
Boehme, J., 53
Bohr, N., 24, 25, 111n, 125n
Boltzmann, L., 114n
Boodin, J.E., 125n
Bosanquet, B., 19, 113n
Boutroux, É., 14, 129n
Bradley, F.H., 19, 29, 106n, 113n,
  121n, 127n
Brentano, F., 116n
Bridgman, P.W., 114n

*Prepared by publisher

Broglie, L. de, 110n
Brunner, E., 3

Carlyle, T., 106n
Cassirer, E., 21, 22, 110n, 120n,
  122n
Cohen, H., 40, 101, 106n

Dakin, A.H., 132n
Dannhouser, W. 122n
D'Abro, A., 114n
Darwin, C., 123n
Dewey, J., 20, 110n, 115n, 116n
Descartes, 6, 9, 10, 101, 107n,
  108n, 109n, 116n, 127n
Dilthey, W., 14, 30
Duns Scotus, J., 117n

Eckhardt, Meister, 53, 54
Eddington, A.S., 26, 31, 107n,
  110n, 112n, 114n
*Efodi* (Duran, P.), 131n
Ehrenfels, C.F. von, 123n
Einstein, A., 25, 27, 31, 67n, 111n,
  112n, 113n, 114n, 125n
Eucken, R.C., 14
Euclid, 9, 23, 105n, 126n

Fechner, G.T., 67
Fichte, J.G., 40, 126n
France, A., 128n